Chronicle Intimacies

By

J S Raynor

Published by Dolman Scott Ltd

ISBN 978-1-909204-01-0

Dolman Scott
www.dolmanscott.com

CONTENTS

CHAPTER ONE - APRIL, 1991 1

CHAPTER TWO - MAY, 1991 11

CHAPTER THREE - JUNE, 1991 30

CHAPTER FOUR - JULY, 1991 47

CHAPTER FIVE - AUGUST, 1991 51

CHAPTER SIX - SEPTEMBER, 1991 57

CHAPTER SEVEN - OCTOBER, 1991 64

CHAPTER EIGHT - NOVEMBER, 1991 67

CHAPTER NINE - DECEMBER, 1991 86

CHAPTER TEN - JANUARY, 1992 108

CHAPTER ELEVEN - FEBRUARY, 1992 116

CHAPTER TWELVE - MARCH, 1992 125

CHAPTER THIRTEEN - APRIL, 1992 132

CHAPTER FOURTEEN - MAY, 1992 141

CHAPTER FIFTEEN - JUNE, 1992 158

CHAPTER SIXTEEN - JULY, 1992 164

CHAPTER SEVENTEEN - AUGUST, 1992 172

A message from John Raynor, the author 191

Epilogue 192

CHAPTER ONE - APRIL, 1991

The introduction agency had, so far, been a dismal failure for me. I did realise that it would be an uphill battle, considering my profile. As soon as a potential partner saw the words, "Registered Blind", there was little reason for them to continue reading my details. To be absolutely honest with myself, why should any woman want to date a blind man? After a few months without any response, I spoke to the owner of the agency and asked if my profile could be amended to omit this detracting fact. I told her that if a potential match was found, I would make them aware of my situation before meeting. I just felt that it would give me a slightly better chance of making contacts. Surprisingly, she agreed, accepting my reasoning.

I was elated when, at last I had a response. From her profile, Marie sounded of interest to me and I hoped that, at last, my loneliness might be coming to an end, two years after splitting up from my first wife. Two seemingly-long years of hard work, but little pleasure as I missed the touch, smell and intimacies of having a woman in my life. The only drawback was Marie's address, which was quite a distance from Manchester. Unfortunately, she lived in the Republic of Ireland. When I eventually plucked up the courage to phone, I found her voice and character pleasant and receptive. We talked for a while, informing each other of our backgrounds. I felt it was too early to mention my eyesight problem at that stage and just enjoyed our conversation, as we appeared to have quite a lot in common.

It came as a blow, when a few days later, I received an angry letter from Marie. After our conversation, she had looked at my profile again and noticed that the agency had clumsily obliterated an entry with Tippex. It had not been completely obscured and she managed, from this, to understand my visual handicap. She phoned the agency and complained about the deception. Obviously, Marie wanted nothing further to do with me. I did send her a letter of apology and hoped that she would understand my reasons.

It did make me feel guilty and I realised that my idea was selfish and, as a consequence, decided to correct the information. After asking the agent to put the words "Registered blind" back in my profile, I did not expect to have any further responses. I always looked closely through the list of potential partners sent from the agency and was surprised to find someone who matched my preferences and, thankfully, did not live too far away. Forty-four year old divorcee, Carol Beeham lived in Mold, North Wales. My spirits raised in anticipation, I asked the agency to pass my details to Carol and waited. To my relief, she responded within just a few days, allowing the agency to reveal her phone number.

I had to pluck up considerable courage to make that most important, first phone call and felt like a nervous teenager, as my call was answered. Her voice was warm and, for once, I felt that my life may be about to turn for the better.

After a few minutes of polite, general conversation, I asked, "Carol, do you like going to the theatre?"

"Yes, actually I do, John. What do you have in mind?"

"There's Phantom of the Opera at the Palace Theatre in Manchester, at the moment. Would you like to see it this coming Saturday?"

She paused for thought. "Yes, I could enjoy that. I'd like to know a bit more about you before I meet you, though."

For the next few minutes, we learned more about each other's backgrounds and I did not find anything about her which changed my mind. At last, I was talking to a woman of warmth and sincerity.

There was something about her which I knew instinctively, even before meeting her for a date, was very special. I did not know what it was, but I knew I must see her. Probably the biggest obstacle to our friendship would be the distance between us. Mold is about forty miles distant from Sale and I did not drive. Still, it was a great deal closer than Southern Ireland where Marie lived, a fact worth taking into account.

This was the part of the conversation I had dreaded with other potential dates. I was worried that she may react in the same way as Marie, but, when I mentioned my eyesight problem, I was relieved to find that Carol was still willing to meet me. The next few days were spent in eager anticipation of our first date. I had suggested that we could go to a restaurant first for a meal and then on to the theatre, but there was a flaw in my planning. Most good restaurants did not start serving meals before six-thirty and the curtain up time was seven-thirty. Since I had never liked to rush things, I realised that this suggestion was not practical.

I had an idea - a solution to my problem. I phoned Carol and asked if she would let me make a meal for her at my house. I knew there was a good chance she may refuse, since, at this stage, she knew very little about me and certainly would not know whether I could be trusted. All the advice on meeting potential partners for the first time suggested meeting in open, public places to avoid difficult, dangerous situations.

"Yes, that would be lovely, John" she answered, to my great surprise and relief. "What time would you like me to be there?"

"Between five and five-thirty should be alright. I'll send a map in the post to give you an idea of the best route." At that time, I did not have her address, but, she gave me this information without hesitation. I wrote her a short letter enclosing the map and joked about her being brave enough to sample my cooking. I had made my own meals for the last two years, but would it be good enough for a guest?

When Saturday, the day of our first meeting, arrived, I was far more nervous than I could remember and felt like a teenager having his first date. I spent most of the day organising myself, cleaning the house, preparing the meal of meat and potato pie and making certain that I was clean and tidy. It was planned like a military operation and, apart from an unexpected phone call, everything went smoothly.

Carol arrived on time and the meal was ready to serve, with the smell of baking pastry meeting her as I opened the door. "I've brought a bottle of wine to have with the meal", she said politely.

I had already opened a bottle of wine and left it to chill in the fridge. "Thanks, Carol. Would you mind if we save this and drink one I have in the fridge?"

"No, not at all." I realised later that I had made a mistake of etiquette. She had quite rightly brought a bottle of red wine, since we were having a meat dish. The plain truth was that I knew chilled white wine was wrong for the meal, but, at that time, I had a distinct preference for white wine. Although I was still very nervous, I found her presence comfortable and my impression of her over the phone proved to be correct. She was a warm and friendly woman and I was happy that she had accepted my date. In appearance, she was everything I could have hoped for and I could not believe my luck at having found someone who matched my ideals so closely. She was about five feet three tall and slim, with short, dark brown hair. Her voice was soft, warm and without any obvious accent or dialect.

"Please have a seat, Carol. I'll just go and put the dinner out."

While I was in the kitchen serving the food, she wandered through and said, "Do you mind if I watch?"

"Er..I'm a bit self-conscious," I stammered awkwardly. As soon as I said it, I wished I had not said something so stupid. I felt terrible as she returned to the dining-room and told myself to be more thoughtful with my future conversation. We both enjoyed the meal and Carol seemed to have a good appetite. The conversation was polite as one might expect on a first meeting. For sweet, I had bought a ready-made raspberry trifle and this soon disappeared as we hungrily attacked it.

After only a short while, Carol had realised that my eyesight was worse than I had implied on the phone. There was no way I could avoid this, no matter how much I tried. I cursed myself for having to conceal the degree of my handicap, but, from past experience, I knew that the only way to avoid natural prejudice was to gain the confidence of the other person first and then show them that I was capable of living a perfectly normal life. I had been registered blind since nineteen seventy nine and although I had no sight at all in my right eye, there was still some useful residual vision in my left. With this, I managed, though I could not pretend that it was easy. Anything left out of place could result in me tripping over it or banging my shins.

After the meal, I piled all the dishes in the kitchen sink and, unusually for me, left them there. I normally washed all dishes straight after use, but, on this occasion, I did not want to waste precious time. We sat in the lounge, talked quite happily and finished the bottle of wine. Although Carol had driven to my house, I had arranged for a taxi to take us to the theatre. I felt this would be better than driving into a city centre she did not know and trying to find somewhere to park. The journey did not take long and we were soon sitting in our circle seats, at the Palace Theatre, eating the chocolates I had bought her.

I felt an excitement I had not felt for years. It was not sexual; more just pleasure that someone was actually with me out of their own choice. For once in my life, I felt my confidence and self-esteem uplifted. “Phantom of the Opera” was excellent and we both seemed to enjoy each other’s company. I had arranged for a taxi to collect us from the theatre, but the show had finished earlier than expected, giving us no choice but to wait ten minutes in the theatre doorway. It was then that I plucked up courage and took hold of Carol’s hand to show her my appreciation of her company. Her hand was warm and soft and, although it might have seemed like the act of a teenager and not a middle-aged man, I did not feel at all self-conscious.

I held her hand for the whole of the journey home and, by

this time, we were both more at ease with each other. I knew once we arrived back at my house that I could not offer her any alcohol, since she would have to drive to her own home before very long. Instead, I offered her a drink of coffee which she accepted gratefully. Again, we talked for a while until she said she had better start making her way home. I knew that I wanted to kiss her, but wondered how she would react. Would she offer her cheek or let me kiss her full on the lips?

"May I kiss you goodnight?" I asked politely. She responded by letting me hold her close and kissing her full on her soft, moist lips. After several tender, lingering kisses, I knew that this was to become a very special relationship. The way she kissed, yielding to my touch, yet responding equally well, gave me great sense of satisfaction, stirring deep emotions within me. How a woman responds to a kiss tells a lot about her feelings. Firm, un-responsive lips suggests a woman who is prepared to be kissed, yet offers little in return. This was not the case with Carol. Her response showed that she was ready to give love as well as receiving it.

Carol was a very warm, tender, responsive woman who I knew I must see again. As I watched her drive away from my house, I had a very happy feeling in my heart and a new-found peace of mind. That night, I slept soundly, feeling very happy and comfortable with the world. Re-living the events of this first date, I felt certain that I walked around with a smile on my face all day Sunday.

I did not know then just when I would be able to see Carol again, but a stroke of luck made it sooner than I had expected. My secretary, Kate, had booked tickets to see 'The King and I' at the Opera House in Manchester for the following Saturday. During the week, she realised that she would not be able to use these tickets and offered them to me. I phoned Carol and asked if she would like to go with me to the theatre again. To my surprise and relief, she immediately accepted. She would not be able to come to my house as early, this time, but would eat a quick meal before starting her journey.

When she arrived at a quarter to seven, I gave her a welcoming hug and a kiss. We only had a few minutes to wait before the taxi arrived to take us the six mile journey to the theatre. We had not finished the box of chocolates from the previous week and took them with us. Our seats were on the front row of the stalls, giving us a really close view of the show. Susan Hampshire played the leading role, in what proved to be a popular production of 'The King and I'. For the whole of the performance, we entwined our arms together, keeping our bodies as close as possible while still sitting in two separate seats. At times, I would run my fingers gently over her palm and even this simple action seemed to excite her as she would arch her palm back in obvious pleasure. Her reactions, in turn, excited me to an extent I could not remember having felt before. My breathing and heart rate were much faster than normal and I had an erection for most of the performance.

Again, after the show, I had arranged for a taxi to take us back to my house. She leaned against me in the taxi and seemed to feel very comfortable in my company. I did not feel inhibited by the presence of the taxi driver and felt certain that he would be used to lovers' passions being aroused in the back of his car. The journey back to Sale seemed to pass very quickly. After arriving home we had a drink of coffee and then started kissing again. The hot, steamy kisses were longer and deeper than ever before and both our bodies shivered with excitement as the passion grew ever more intense. She shrugged her jacket off, allowing me to lift her jumper and touch her breasts gently. They were small, but firm breasts and extremely responsive to my caresses. Our sighs of mutual pleasure were the only sounds to be heard as we held each other close and continued our petting and passionate kisses.

"What do you want?" she whispered enticingly.

"I want to make love to you." I had surprised myself. I never imagined events to move so fast.

Her response surprised me. "I want you inside me. But not here - let's go upstairs." I could not believe my ears. Nobody had ever said that they actually wanted me before. Even the word 'want' was like music to my ears. Was this a seduction, and, if so, who was seducing who? I led her out of the lounge and moved towards the stairs. "Don't switch the lights off." I had switched them off as a natural thing to do on leaving a room, but I think I understood the symbolic reasons for her making this request. As soon as we entered my bedroom and closed the curtains, she began to take her clothes off. I followed suit but took longer to reach the same state of undress. As I had not anticipated having a sexual experience this early in the relationship, I was not prepared, having no condoms and hoped this would not interfere too much in our activities. I had not made love for several years and desperately hoped that I could satisfy her desires. I knew that I must be sexually more naive than Carol. In fact, not many men could be as sexually inexperienced as me since I only had one previous sexual partner, my ex-wife. As Carol lay on the bed, my penis showed my level of arousal. It was hot, stiff and very big as she opened her legs and gently eased it into her soft, moist vagina. "Don't come inside me," she said quietly. "I don't want you to make me pregnant." I knew that this had to be very special love-making and not something to rush. I made long, slow movements of my body and Carol responded far better than I could have expected. Her orgasmic sighs were loud and very intense. She gained particular pleasure when I sucked her breasts. We made love for at least an hour and a half, with Carol having several orgasms and, although I did not come at all, It did not bother me as I had gained so much enjoyment from giving her so much pleasure. The fact I had not ejaculated might have been as a result of the fear of an unwanted pregnancy, but I really did not mind. The beauty of it all was that my poor vision had not impaired the evening at all. In fact, it may well have enhanced it since my sense of touch was now more acute than ever. The only reference made to it was when Carol lay naked on the bed, looked up at me and asked if I could see her clearly. My level of vision meant that close objects were reasonably clear though not sharply defined, while far objects were much more difficult to distinguish.

In Carol's case, I could see quite clearly her welcome smile, her boyish features and the flowing curves of her body. The one thing I had to admit was that I could not tell what colour her eyes were. I did know they were hazel, but, try as I might, I could not see the colour.

"I've never known anyone as gentle as you, darling. I don't like leaving you like this, but I am going to have to go shortly - It's nearly one o'clock and, much as I would love to, I can't stay for the night."

"I wish you could, but don't worry. I do understand and I will be alright." Carol dressed while I lay naked on the bed watching her. "I'll come downstairs to see you off," I said as she pulled her jacket on and was ready for leaving.

"You'd better put something on", she said with a smile as she looked at my still erect penis. She handed me my housecoat which I slipped on and then followed her downstairs. I gave her one final, lingering kiss and watched her walk to her car.

"Please drive carefully love, and phone me when you get home."

"Don't worry, John. I'll take it easy." As her car disappeared into the distance, I went back into my house and gave a sigh of happiness. I lay on my bed for a while re-living the memories of the evening and felt exhilarated that such a passionate woman actually wanted me. My pubic area ached from my exertions, but I did not mind at all. I could not remember a time when I had managed to maintain an erection for so long. After a while, I went and stayed at the side of the telephone waiting for Carol's call. Just fifty minutes after leaving my house, she phoned. Carol sounded very happy and I knew that we had formed a relationship that night which was out of this world. We did not talk for long as we were both tired and wished each other a good night's sleep.

Although I fell asleep fairly quickly, I awoke at about four o'clock, feeling very thirsty and hungry, which was most unusual for me. If I did not satisfy my appetite, I knew I would find it difficult to fall asleep again. After a few minutes, debating what to do, I went downstairs and raided the fridge. A drink and snack were sufficient to satisfy my hunger and I returned to my bed, where I slept soundly for several more hours.

When I awoke that Sunday morning, I felt that the world was such a beautiful place. The memories of the night before flooded back and yet I still had difficulty believing it had actually happened. Just the fact that someone wanted me made me feel so good and happy with the world. My pubic area still ached, but, in a way, the fact that our passionate activities had brought pain excited me all the more, although I would not wish the same upon Carol.

For the rest of that day, I must have walked around in a day-dream. I knew I must see her again, but had to be careful not to be too demanding on her time. I still did not know much about Carol and her family commitments. I did know that she had two teenage boys, Peter and Martin. We spoke to each other on the phone after that weekend and, I was elated to be able to arrange for me to meet her in Chester, two weeks later.

CHAPTER TWO - MAY, 1991

I was like a small boy looking forward to Christmas. My secretary, Kate knew of our date and commented on my new-found happiness. Those two weeks, those fourteen days seemed to pass ever so slowly. When that long-awaited Saturday finally arrived, I decided to dress casually, though, hopefully still looking reasonably smart. On our first two dates, I had worn a suit and tie, but felt that, for this day, beige slacks, white trainers, white sports shirt and casual jacket would be more appropriate. I put plenty of my Chanel after-shave on, combed my hair into what would, hopefully, look reasonable for a man in his forties.

As I walked along the platform after alighting from the train at Chester, Carol saw me, walked up and gave me a big hug and kiss. I was pleased that she did not mind showing her affection in public, since the inhibitions of my earlier life had now disappeared. We walked out of the station hand in hand and headed for Carol's car. Once in the car, we kissed and cuddled before driving to another part of the city. Carol knew of a car park close to the city wall, where we could leave the car for a few hours. Once there, we walked around the wall, for most of the time holding hands, and talked of our past lives.

Carol had been divorced for a few years after an affair with a married man. This disclosure immediately raised many questions in my mind, which I dare not ask. What had become of this other man and what were Carol's feelings for him now? If she had chosen to answer my questions, I probably would not have liked the answers she may have given. I did know that, although this other man might still be in the background somewhere, it would not affect my feelings for Carol, nor must it spoil our enjoyment of each other. After all, if she had any strong attachment to this man, then she would not have joined an introduction agency and accepted my date.

I told her of my own marriage, of how my wife and I had simply drifted apart over the years and how this resulted in our separation and subsequent divorce. I found something very comforting about Carol's company and it was not just sexual anticipation.

Although Carol knew the area well, she was not aware of the Water Tower, which was obviously intended as a tourist attraction. We went up the few steps into the reception area where, after paying our entrance fee, we were each handed a small, electronic receiver which was designed to hang around our necks. The first room we entered was darkened and, through lenses mounted in the roof of the tower, an image of the surrounding area was projected on to a horizontal white board in the centre of the room. After looking at this for a few minutes, I pulled Carol close to me and gave her a deep, passionate kiss. I imagined us making love in that strange room, but knew it was not a practical idea. This was proven as we separated on hearing someone else climbing the stairs.

We then walked down some more steps to a circular room with several alcoves around its perimeter. Through small earphones attached to our receivers, we were able to hear a different, dramatised commentary in each alcove. We both agreed that it had been very cleverly designed and sat in every alcove, holding each other close while we listened to this potted history of Chester. The next stop after the water tower was a bar, near to the river, where Carol had an extra dry Martini and I had a whisky and soda. The bar was not very pleasant and the service was slow, but at least it provided us with some refreshment on a warm, May day.

Eventually, we reached the end of our journey around the wall and headed back towards Carol's car. She drove to a car park near to the theatre and, from there we walked to a small restaurant off the first floor walk-way so typical of Chester. This was where I had to admit to Carol that my eyesight was not good enough to read the menu. I felt so useless at having to ask my partner to read to me. She did not seem to mind, but I knew that this would trigger off many questions about the extent of my vision.

Carol had asked if I would sit opposite her at the table, rather than by her side and, after a while, she asked, "Can you see me clearly, darling?"

"Yes, I can see you quite well, because the lighting in here is fairly good, but there are so many factors which determine how well I see, that it is difficult to explain." I knew that this was not a completely satisfactory answer, but found great difficulty in comparing vision with anyone else, since my eyesight had never been good. From birth, I never had any vision in my right eye and that of my left had deteriorated gradually over the years through a condition known as retinitis pigmentosa. In everybody's eyes, there are millions of light sensitive cells on the retina. In a person with normal eyesight, these cells are constantly dying off and being regenerated, but, in my case, no new cells are being created. This results in a gradual blurring of vision as more 'dead spots' appear on the retina.

I knew this could eventually lead to total blindness, but also knew there was no point in dwelling on this probability. It was far preferable, I felt, to get on with life and not to let it spoil my enjoyment of the world and everything in it. I had to accept that this unwanted inheritance would make me less attractive to women and, since I was certainly not handsome, my chances of attracting anyone were extremely remote.

This made it all the more incredible that I was now with a woman who obviously had fairly strong feelings for me. Equally, my feelings for her were already very strong and I found her warm, attractive, good company and very desirable. As she smiled at me across the table, I felt such a thrill and thanked God that fate had brought us together.

In making our choice from the menu, we each chose a different starter, allowing us to share them. We sat at that table happily feeding each other, completely oblivious to anyone else in the restaurant. Carol kept me sexually aroused for the whole of the meal, by stroking her bare toes up and down my legs. This simple action meant so much to me that I felt quite overcome with emotion. As with the first course, we chose different sweets with the intention of again sharing them. When the waitress brought them, she asked who was having which sweet. Carol and I looked at each other with a questioning smile.

The waitress understood our looks and said with a knowing smile, “Ah, you’re sharing them, are you? We nodded in acknowledgement just as if we were two, small children and once again, spoon-fed each other. It would have been very obvious to anyone watching us that we were lovers, but neither of us felt the slightest inhibitions.

We had taken our time over the meal, so that we could walk straight from the restaurant to the theatre in good time for the start of the performance. On this occasion, Carol had chosen the theatre and booked tickets. The small theatre was quite full for the play about an Italian couple whose marriage was destroyed when the husband had an affair. Carol commented that the theme was a bit too near the truth for comfort, but I restrained myself from asking any probing questions. Although I was curious about her relationships, I was determined that I would let Carol tell me what she wanted and in her own time.

We did follow the play, but derived more pleasure from each other’s company. We held each other close, petted and enjoyed the occasional passionate kiss. The fact that the people around us could see our obvious displays of affection for each other did not bother us at all.

After the show, we walked around Chester for just a little while and then returned to Carol’s car. It was ten-thirty and Carol had booked a taxi for eleven o’clock, to take me home. We decided to take advantage of the remaining time to enjoy each other within Carol’s car. Since we were in a car park in the centre of Chester, there was a limit to what we could get up to without being observed, but, short of actual intercourse, we took full advantage of the time available to us. Carol had very sensitive breasts and derived great enjoyment, as indeed I did, from holding each other close, bare breasts to bare breasts. As I fondled her, she sighed with erotic pleasure and said, "Oh, darling, I want you to do that all night. As soon as we can have the whole night together, please do that for me."

These words were both surprising and magical to my ears. The thought of spending the whole night with Carol increased my excitement and I replied, "I will, my darling, I will." The experience of being so intimate in a car and, in what really was a public place, was yet another first for me. As a middle-aged man, as I had to admit I was, I was now experiencing what most teenagers took for granted, many of them going the whole way within their car. I still had difficulty in believing that this was really happening to me. It must be a beautiful dream from which I had yet to wake up at some stage and, yet, everything was so real. The warmth of Carol's slender body, her deep, intense kisses, the darkness of the night, the sound of people walking nearby was all too realistic to be just a dream.

That thirty minutes passed far too quickly and, when my taxi arrived, we gave one last, lingering kiss and then parted company. On the journey home, I ran through all the events of that day over and over in my mind. I knew that my feelings for Carol were getting stronger with each meeting, each kiss and each touch. Was it sexual or something much deeper? I had not set out to fall in love and certainly never expected to fall so quickly. Everything about Carol felt so right. She was slim, petite, intelligent, very warm hearted and had many interests in common with me. I realised that it must be love when I found that she was constantly in my thoughts from awakening in the morning until falling asleep last thing at night. I looked forward even to the sound of her voice on the telephone. It had such warmth and sincerity that I could never tire of hearing her voice.

Before I met Carol, I had booked to go to Paris for a short holiday and now wished I had not. I asked Carol if she would be able to go with me, but I knew what the answer would be.

"I can't, love. There's no way I can leave the children - not for that length of time."

Occasionally, the children did stay with Carol's ex-husband, Alan, but that was usually for only one night. "You go on your holiday, darling, and we'll see each other soon after you get back."

The following Friday, I took a taxi to Manchester Airport and made my way to the information desk. Since I was now unable to read signs and notices, I had discovered that the best way to enjoy a holiday, was to inform the airport of the potential difficulties and they would provide assistance. I hated drawing attention to myself and my visual impairment, but, if it was done with a little sensitivity, a personal courier through the airports was, by far, the best solution. This type of assistance did not mean that security was relaxed and I was thoroughly frisked as I was passing through the area where hand luggage is checked. I did not mind this, since they had taken my word for it that I had anything wrong with my eyes. My escort, a pretty young woman, chatted quite happily as we went through the airport and she did not leave me until I was safely in my seat on the DC-10. Throughout the short, uneventful flight, the stewardesses were attentive and helpful. I did realise that, if Carol had gone with me, none of this special treatment would have been provided, but I would have forsaken it all for the chance to be with her. I knew that a few, romantic days in Paris with Carol would have been perfect, but this was not to be possible.

At Charles De Gaulle airport, another pretty, young escort joined me at the aircraft and made the process of passing through customs and baggage collection so easy. She spoke English with a delightful accent and I felt in a good holiday mood, ready for whatever the next few days had in store for me. She found a taxi to take me to my hotel and wished me a pleasant holiday.

I had never been to France before and could not speak the

language, but had bought a 'When in France' cassette a few weeks earlier. The few words and phrases I had learned in that short space of time would, I hoped, be sufficient to make myself understood and find my way around. This was based on the assumption that many French people could speak English. My expectations, however, were a little bit too high and only the occasional person, such as the hotel receptionist, was willing to converse in my native language.

This did make things a little more difficult, since I had to rely on my memory rather than resort to phrase-books or maps. The hotel room was quite small and basic in terms of quality, but it served the purpose. I vowed to myself that, if I was fortunate to take Carol to a hotel, it would have to be of much better quality.

On my first afternoon in Paris, I thought I should explore the area after settling in at my hotel. I found a major road with many shops and cafes not far from my hotel and spent a while walking around and looking for landmarks. When hunger gained the better of me, I chose one of the many cafes and entered, hoping that I could avoid ordering something I did not like. As I sat at a table near the window, a waitress, wearing a brightly coloured skirt and very low-cut blouse approached and offered me a menu. I asked if she spoke English and quickly discovered that she did not. She soon realised that the most sensible idea would be to find someone else who could understand me. Another similarly dressed waitress appeared from the kitchen and helped me to choose my meal using a very broken form of English.

After a quite enjoyable, though not very filling meal, I felt confident enough to walk a bit further away. The first thing I had to do was find a large landmark. Near to my hotel, there was a metro station and I felt that this was big enough to use. My plan was to walk a rectangular route with the entrance to the metro forming one of the short sides. It was when I was trying to complete the rectangle that I went wrong. The streets in that area of Paris were anything but parallel and, as a result, unknown to me, I was getting further away from my starting point.

When I did not recognise any of the surrounding areas, I realised my mistake and felt extremely stupid at being lost on my first day in Paris. I was not particularly worried, since I knew that I could not be a great distance from my hotel and just needed to find a taxi to get back. Eventually, I discovered a cab, but was charged over the odds when the driver realised I was English. I would have to be better organised for the rest of the holiday.

On the Saturday morning, a coach with a well-spoken Tourist guide collected me from my hotel and took me on a conducted tour of the main sights of Paris such as the Eiffel Tower, Arc de Triumph, Notre Dame and the usual tourist attractions. While it was interesting, I did find the sheer volume of tourists spoiled the experience. Still, I was, myself, one of those many thousands of tourists eager to see France's capital city, so I could not complain too much. I had made friends with an American on the coach and found it useful to stay with him if only to make certain that I could find my way back to the coach.

In the afternoon, I went shopping with a mission in mind. Whatever else I did while in France, I was determined to buy a present for Carol. She was constantly in my thoughts and I missed her desperately. I really wanted to give her something which she could treasure for many years. When I became lost the day before, I had noticed a large shopping area, but this time I made certain I could retrace my route. I found a shopping arcade in a building which housed a metro station and spent a while scouring the area for the right type of store.

After a difficult time, trying to determine which kind of shops I was passing, I found a little lingerie shop called 'Sylva' and nervously entered. I felt certain that someone here would speak English, but to my dismay, found this not to be the case. I felt that my limited knowledge of the language was insufficient and left the shop empty-handed. Thinking that I might stand a better chance in a department store, I walked a few blocks away, making a careful mental note of the numbers of crossings and corners. I found a huge store and felt certain they would have a lingerie section. The thing I did not anticipate was the size of the shopping complex I had just entered. It was spread over several blocks, each connected by high-level enclosed bridges. This made the task of finding what I wanted even more difficult and I had visions of getting lost within this marble and glass maze. Worse still, I could not find any assistants who spoke English. After a while of walking along endless passageways, I gave up and decided to leave the store. I still do not know whether it was good luck or management, but I succeeded in finding the entrance door from which I had started my tour.

I made my way back to Sylva's in the hope that I could make myself understood. When I entered the shop, I caught sight of an advert on the counter. It was of a woman dressed only in bra and knickers. When the young woman assistant had finished attending to her previous customer, she showed recognition at seeing this curious Englishman again. I pointed to the knickers in the advert. At last, she understood - sign language still has its uses. She asked, again by pointing, what colour of knickers I wished to buy. Black was my choice. She then spread several pairs on the counter, allowing me to make my selection. After a few minutes of indecision, I finally chose one very sexy pair and handed them to the assistant. She realised the importance of presentation of my purchase and spent several minutes gift wrapping the knickers. I thanked her for her help and happily left the shop with the parcel inside a neat little carrier bag advertising Sylva's.

I headed back for my hotel and, miraculously, found my way without too much difficulty. On my journey, I met a couple of English women who were lost and even managed to help them find their way back. Their hotel was on the same street as mine, the Rue de Berne. We parted company and I entered my own hotel, where I had a shower and change of clothes. I felt that I should try and find a better restaurant for my evening meal and asked the receptionist for advice. He told me that the local restaurants were not very good and said that, if I could wait until seven o'clock when he was off duty, he could show me an excellent place to eat.

A few minutes later, another guest asked much the same question. He was from New Zealand and was with his wife and daughter. At seven, we all followed the receptionist, while he led us a somewhat tortuous route for about twenty minutes, until we, at last, arrived at a very pleasant restaurant. By this time, I was chatting quite happily to the New Zealand family and was asked if I would join them for the meal. I was very grateful for the company and enjoyed a superb dinner. By the end of the evening, we had made good friends of them and they had invited me to visit and stay at their house in New Zealand. I did not know whether I would be able to take advantage of the offer, but greatly appreciated their gesture. Back at the hotel, I talked for quite a while to the helpful receptionist, making arrangements for the rest of my holiday.

Sunday morning was spent quietly, walking just within a few blocks of my hotel. A coach arrived in the afternoon to take me to the Palace of Versailles. When I saw the magnificent extravagances of this period of history, I could understand the reasons for the Revolution. Within a few minutes of arriving at the Palace, I had found a charming English couple from Cheshire. We got on quite well and stayed together for the tour of the Palace and its gardens. For some strange reason, I had found it much easier to make friends since my separation. I certainly found it quite easy to make conversation and was, I suppose, less inhibited than I would have been with my former spouse.

After an enjoyable afternoon, I returned to my hotel to prepare for my evening's entertainment. With a shower, a clean shave and my most presentable suit, I felt ready for whatever the evening may have in store for me. At seven thirty an empty, forty seater luxury coach arrived at my hotel and I was the only person to be collected. As I relaxed in the comfort of the wide seats, this sleek, impressive monster glided through the narrow streets of Paris, stopping at several hotels to pick up other guests. When everybody had been collected, the coach was still only about half full, but it then made its way to the embankment of the river Seine.

The passengers were escorted to a boarding point where we went aboard a wide, modern river cruiser. Our English-speaking courier escorted us to our appropriate dinner table. Many tables were already occupied and the air was filled with the chatter of the cruiser's occupants. A complimentary glass of pink champagne was offered to each guest and, in my case, I had two glasses. I had met a very pleasant couple from Boston, USA, on the coach and they were sitting opposite me at the table. I had the impression that they were newly-weds and the young woman offered me her champagne. It struck me that she was being quite sensible in avoiding too much alcohol, assuming she wished to remain reasonably sober.

I was probably the only person on board without a partner and felt particularly sad that Carol was not with me to enjoy this romantic, candle-lit dinner while cruising on the Seine. The newly-weds were sitting side by side, opposite me and I thought it prudent not to disturb their enjoyment of each other by talking too much to them. Apart from anything else, the level of noise on board, just from people talking, was too much to hear conversation across the wide table. Another couple on the other side of me had made the mistake of sitting opposite each other, making it difficult for them to converse. It was the woman who was sitting next to me and we soon found it very easy to talk to each other. This helped to reduce the feelings of loneliness I had earlier experienced. It took a while for everyone to be served and for the cruiser to start its journey. I think part of the delay was deliberate to ensure darkness before leaving its mooring. Powerful floodlights were attached to both sides of the cruiser and these were projecting large pools of light onto the river banks. Since the inside of the cruiser was now lit only by candle-light, the effect of the reflections of the floodlights on banks, bridges and the river itself were quite stunning to both occupants and onlookers. A small jazz band on board provided background music for the evening, which added even more to the overall effect.

During the conversation with Sherry, the woman sitting at the side of me, she became aware of my poor eyesight. As a result, she was really helpful in pointing out the landmarks I had difficulty making out. The good food, wine and good company made that evening one of the most unforgettable of my life. I was, by this stage, quite intoxicated from the effects of both the champagne and wine, but still quite coherent. After a sweet of nougat and fresh raspberries and a drink of cognac, I felt very comfortable and relaxed. At about eleven-thirty, the cruiser arrived back at its starting point and all passengers disembarked. I thanked Sherry for being such good company and, with a squeeze of her hand, wished her goodnight. Our original courier directed the American couple, myself and several others back to the coach we had arrived in earlier that evening. It then made more calls at other hotels in Paris, picking up more passengers. When all the passengers had been collected, the coach headed out of the city.

I was already feeling quite tired, even though there was more entertainment to come. When I had organised my excursions, the receptionist had told me of several cabaret night spots. I had asked for his recommendations and he said that the Crazy Horse had the reputation of being the most erotic in Paris. Since I may never get the opportunity again, I had decided to opt for the Crazy Horse in preference to the Moulin Rouge or the Lido. To our surprise, we all had to stand on the pavement outside a very ordinary looking building for at least twenty minutes. I had the impression that the timing had been miscalculated and we were waiting for the end of the previous performance.

Eventually, we were allowed to enter the club and led into a fairly small auditorium with seating arranged as in a theatre. There was more than usual space between the seating and shelves were attached to the back of each seat to provide space for a glass and ash-tray. The young couple from Boston were sitting at the side of me and we all wondered what the show would be like. Our courier told us that, within the price of the ticket, each person was allowed two free drinks. He gave us a warning that, if we chose either wine or champagne, there would be an additional charge and it would be expensive.

Not wanting to miss the opportunity for a free drink, or, at least, drinks I had already paid for, I chose a whisky and dry ginger. The taking of orders and serving of drinks did seem to take a long time and, all the time, there was just background music playing, but the curtains remained closed.

While sitting there in a strange night club in the early hours of the morning in Paris, I began to wonder just what I was doing there. Would I have gone there if Carol had been with me? No, I'm certain that we would not have gone there together. I also knew that I was not a middle-aged man who liked to ogle near-naked women. A fear that is increasing in strength, the older I become, is the possible complete loss of eyesight. It is this very fear that is driving me to travel and gain new experiences while I am still able to see them, even though the images would be somewhat blurred. I know that I am fortunate in being able to afford to satisfy these urges.

At long last, the curtains opened to reveal a fairly small stage. Several long-legged, scantily clad girls began to dance to what seemed to me to be very loud recorded music. Much use was made of projected pictures on to a screen behind the girls to create different backgrounds. The dancing was fairly suggestive though, I must admit; I did not find it the least bit erotic. I suppose it could have been described as

artistic, but I felt a certain amount of disappointment. I did realise that I might be missing some of the effect with my restricted vision, but I certainly could not ask the American couple to describe what was happening.

The big mistake I did make was to have too much to drink. I felt terrible to wake up and discover that I had slept through some of the performance. In a way, it was quite amusing, really, to have slept through what was hailed as one of the most erotic shows in Europe. The night air felt clean and sharp as we left the club to rejoin our courier on the coach. At three-thirty that morning, I arrived back at my hotel feeling very drunk and exhausted. I was not able to sleep late, since I had made arrangements for another special excursion that Monday morning.

After just a few hours of restless sleep I was disturbed by the phone. It was reception with my alarm call. Sleepily, I showered, dressed and ate a brief breakfast. At ten o'clock, I went down to reception and, after a few minutes, a young, dark-haired woman entered the hotel. I went up to her and said, "Good morning. Are you Sonia?"

She looked relieved at having found her client so easily. "Your chauffeur will be here in a few minutes. Until then, perhaps we could discuss your requirements?"

Her grasp of the English language was excellent and, as usual, English spoken with a slight foreign accent sounded much better than that spoken by most British people. After some discussion, we went outside and found the French chauffeur sitting in a brand new Metro. He could not speak any English, but that was not important, since my escort would give him all the instructions.

Sonia produced a map and showed the driver the route to take. I knew this was the best way to see Paris. The receptionist at my hotel had contacted several friends and had managed to find Sonia, a student in her late twenties, who was willing to act as a personal courier. Unfortunately, she did not drive and, for that reason, a chauffeur had to be found. As we were driving around the streets of Paris, Sonia was pointing out some of the landmarks which she felt warranted comment but not interesting enough to stop. I had told Sonia that I did not want to see the usual tourist attractions. I was more interested in feeling the atmosphere of the real Paris and, to this end, we walked through many narrow streets bordering the banks of the Seine. We strolled leisurely through areas where academics gathered and stopped in several small parks. I was still feeling very tired after the previous evening's excursions and was glad of the occasional rest.

We had lunch together in a little cafe which seemed to be frequented only by Parisians. It was a relief not to hear the intrusions of American small talk which seemed to pervade the Paris I had seen before that day. Sonia and I had a good day together, with me asking a great deal of questions and, thanks to her intimate knowledge of the area, she was able to provide answers to most of them. If I had difficulty in making out the detail of some feature she was showing me, she would describe it to me in quite good detail.

I felt sorry for the chauffeur who stayed with his car all day and was always ready to transport us to another area. At one point, we were driving along a wide, busy road with cars passing on either side of us, when I felt a bump on my side of the car as a van passed too close to us. My first thoughts were for the driver's brand new Metro. Both vehicles stopped and the drivers began arguing in loud voices. After a few minutes of letting off steam, they calmed down and agreed that the damage did not warrant any further action. There was not an actual dent as I had expected from the impact. There was a scratch, however, but this could probably be touched up without too much difficulty.

At five o'clock, we arrived at the airport, where I paid the chauffeur using my remaining francs and Sonia with English currency. I thanked them both for a tremendous day and they wished me a safe journey as I entered the airport terminal. It was shortly after this that I had my first upset of the holiday. I gave my name to the woman on the Air Lingus desk and she told me that someone would be along to assist me shortly. A man did arrive and asked me to wait a few minutes and then he would return with a wheelchair. I felt certain I must have misheard him. Why on earth would they want to bring a wheelchair? Then I remembered something I had heard a long time before. I had heard that some French people did not know how to handle someone with a visual handicap and would, in affect, assume them to be an invalid. I had no intention of being humiliated in such a way. I went back to the young woman at the Air Lingus desk, who, I felt certain, would be more sensible. She agreed that a wheelchair was completely un-necessary and said she would have a word with the escort. He still arrived with it, however. I made it very clear to him that I had no intention of sitting in it, and, seeing my annoyance, left the wheelchair behind. He still did not have much idea, though, since he grabbed my arm from behind and tried to push me along. As politely as I could, I explained to him that, if he would walk in front of me and slightly to my left, that was all that was necessary. He nervously kept turning around, presumably to make certain that I had not fallen over. This was the first time of travelling through several airports that I had encountered such ignorance. I had to admit to myself that I did have different rules for male and female escorts. If a woman offered me her hand, I would never refuse it, but my masculinity made me feel very uncomfortable if I had to hold hands with a man.

As I entered the plane, an Irish stewardess greeted me and I said, "That is a very welcome accent, after the last few days." The flight was quick and routine and, thankfully, once I arrived at Manchester airport, a young woman was there to assist me and find my luggage. A short journey by taxi was all that was necessary to reach my home. Returning home after a holiday always seemed to be an anticlimax and I am never certain whether I am sad or glad to be back. The thought of seeing Carol just two days later was enough to convince me I was in the right place.

When Carol arrived on Wednesday night, I greeted her eagerly with a hug and a kiss. We had a drink and some sandwiches and found that we still had plenty of time before the taxi was due to arrive to take us to the theatre. We began kissing passionately and, before long, went upstairs to my bedroom. This time, I was better prepared and had a large supply of condoms at the side of my bed. We quickly stripped off our clothes and made energetic, exquisite and exciting love. We both climaxed at the same time and lay, exhausted and happy, on the bed. We still kissed and cuddled and stroked each other's naked body, losing all track of time and were still lying, enjoying ourselves when the doorbell rang.

The taxi had arrived and neither of us had a stitch of clothing on. "I'll go and ask him to wait a few minutes," Carol said as she began to dress. I was quite amazed at the speed of her dressing.

She was dressed, spoken to the taxi driver and returned upstairs and I still was not ready. "I'll fasten your laces, love" she said patiently. I was fastening my tie while she did my shoe laces.

As Carol was rushing downstairs, I shouted, "Oh, darling, there's some chocolates in the fridge - would you get them, please?" I put the intruder alarm on, locked the doors and tumbled into the taxi, flushed with excitement. The taxi did not take long to reach the theatre.

The show, that evening, was Agatha Christie's Verdict, a clever murder story. The production was designed in such a way that only one stage set was necessary.

We both enjoyed the show and each other. It's surprising that we managed to follow the story, since we held each other close, kissed and petted for the whole performance. I did notice that people sitting on either side of us never asked to pass us and, instead, seemed prepared to go the long way round. Our souls seemed to be intimately entwined in a dream of happiness.

The one flaw to the whole evening occurred when Carol, noticing the lovesick look in my eyes, said "Darling, please don't expect too much of me." I wondered what she was trying to tell me.

True, I had fallen very much in love and far quicker than I had ever imagined possible. The impression Carol had given me was that she, equally, had fallen in love with me. The fact that she had given herself to me completely, held nothing back and the way in which we seemed to melt into each other every time we met helped to reinforce this belief. Was it perhaps the ghost of this other man which was creating some warning, some caution in her mind? Or was it perhaps that the pace of our relationship was frightening her? She even said, shortly after making this request, "I don't know what I'm doing - you're not even my type of man." This comment did hurt and I was puzzled by the reason for the statement.

"What is your type of man?" I asked, uncertain of whether I wanted to hear the answer.

"I don't know. I'm sorry. I do love you, but things seem to be happening too fast. Please just give me time." She gave me a comforting hug and smiled at me to try and allay my worries. I did try and put it to the back of my mind, but it was a warning I could not ignore.

Even the taxi journey home was good with Carol by my side. We held each other close, kissed and petted for the whole journey home. The driver, sensing our mood, played background music from a cassette for us, completing the atmosphere of romance. Back home, we had a drink and talked happily together. I excused myself and ran upstairs, returning a couple of minutes later with a small, gift-wrapped parcel. As I handed it to Carol, I said, smiling, "I've brought a little present for you, from Paris."

She could not miss the 'Sylva's Lingerie' printing on the wrapping and probably realised the contents. Carol gave a delightful smile as she unwrapped the parcel containing the knickers.

"Darling, they're lovely. You're very naughty, you know."

"I suppose I am. You're not offended, though, are you?"

"No. Of course I'm not. At first, when I saw them, I thought, 'how dare he?' but I really do love the thought you've put into my present. As long as you don't expect me to be under any obligation."

"No, that's understood - no obligation. I wanted to bring you something personal and memorable. I knew that I could not get something the children might see, since you don't want them to know about me. I had quite a bit of fun buying those, you know."

"I can imagine." She gave me a long kiss of gratitude and said in a sensuous voice, "I'll wear them next time we meet and you can take them off me." The very thought of this action excited me and I wished we could make love again. What she said next took my breath away. "I do love you, darling. At least, I think I do. Perhaps we should go somewhere for a dirty week.." She quickly corrected herself. "er, somewhere where we can get the sex out of our system and see if there is anything left."

I knew, in my mind, that there was much more than just a physical attraction between us. The chemistry was so right that it would be a crime to do anything else but enjoy each other's company. It had surprised me that she was suggesting basically what she very nearly called it - a dirty weekend. I was not shocked, though and said, "You know I'd love to spend a weekend with you. If that's what you would like, let's do it soon."

"Soon, darling. But I must go, now."

It was late and she was working the following day, so I gave her one last kiss and wished her a safe journey home. If only she could stay for the night, I would have been on top of the world. Making love with Carol was fantastic, but I knew that I wanted her to spend the whole night with me, holding each other close while we slept. I could only hope that this would happen soon.

We talked frequently on the phone, usually late at night, when Carol's children were in bed and, during the next few days, arranged that Carol would come to my house on Saturday, the next weekend. The arrangement was that Carol would bring a frozen meal for two and we would stay in, making as much love as we wanted. The very thought of it excited me and I waited in eager anticipation of that day. Such great sexpectations!

CHAPTER THREE - JUNE, 1991

When Saturday arrived, I went to the shopping centre, as usual, knowing that this routine operation was probably the only one that I would be doing that day. I was in good spirits and chatted happily to the Tesco assistant who was helping me with my shopping. I caught a taxi to carry me and my several bags home. As I reached my front door, I heard the telephone ringing. I rushed to unlock the door, turn off the alarm and throw my shopping into the hallway.

I was desperately hoping that, whoever it was, they would not ring off. As I picked up the receiver, I heard Carol's voice. She was in tears and sobbed, "Oh, darling, I'm sorry, but I can't come today."

My heart had sunk to fathomless depths at these few words, spoken with such trembling emotion. "Why? What's wrong?" As she continued to sob, I said, "Please, darling, don't cry. Please don't cry. What's wrong?" By this time, I was in tears myself.

"I do love you. I really do. But I love someone else even more." This was the last thing I wanted to hear at that moment. Carol explained that the man with whom she had an affair was still her main love. She said that their relationship had been on and off for quite a long time.

Carol had been trying not to see him for a few months, but she still knew that she loved him. She was still in tears as she heard her children walking along her drive. "I must go now - the boys are coming." The phone clicked as she hung up and I was left standing there, holding the phone, feeling devastated and stunned by her revelation. In a matter of seconds, the bottom had fallen out of my world.

I really did not know what to do with myself. Carol meant so much to me that I could not stop the tears flowing as her words kept echoing through my numbed mind. I almost felt ashamed at the strength of my emotions and I was thankful that nobody was there to witness a middle-aged man being reduced to a shaking wreck by his passion for a woman who could no longer return his love.

In a daze of despair, I eventually pulled myself together a little and rinsed my face to ease my stinging eyes. I wearily unpacked my morning's shopping and then slumped again in a chair, incapable of doing anything productive.

Shortly after midday, the phone rang. It could only have been Carol. I answered the phone apprehensively and was relieved to hear Carol's more composed voice. "Darling, I.. I've been thinking what we should do. I won't come to your house, but I want you to meet me somewhere. We can find a hotel and stay the night. Would you like to do that?"

I could not believe my ears. Less than two hours earlier, I thought I had lost Carol, forever. Now, instead of coming to my house for the evening, she was suggesting that we spend the whole night together. I did not understand the logic, but I was not going to reject her idea, since, to me, the very thought of spending the weekend with Carol excited and intrigued me. "You know there is nothing I'd like better. Where would you like to stay? Chester, Manchester?"

"Not Chester. I think somewhere between; perhaps somewhere in the Cheshire countryside. Can you meet me at Knutsford or even Northwich?"

"Yes, of course. I'll meet you anywhere you want. I can phone British Rail and check train times and then ring you back." A few minutes later, I had checked the times and phoned her back. We arranged to meet at Northwich just after three thirty. This new plan spurred me into action and, now feeling blissfully happy, I ate a quick lunch, showered and made myself as presentable as possible. I dressed casually, wearing white trainers, slacks, sports shirt and casual jacket.

As I started my journey, I was very anxious about the possibility of missing my train or, worse still, missing Northwich station. I knew that I sometimes found difficulty in reading the station names and, to assist me, asked British Rail how many stations there would be on my journey. Northwich would be the seventh station from Altrincham.

The train was only a few minutes late and, as I made my journey, my excitement increased with each station I passed. The fourth, fifth, sixth and finally the seventh station came into sight. I peered at the station signs and managed to distinguish the name. Northwich! I had arrived and eagerly stepped off the train. There was nobody on the platform, but realised that the ticket office was on the other platform and so made my way to the foot-bridge. When I reached the top of the steps and looked across the bridge, I saw a solitary figure walking towards me. That familiar smile and delicate figure could belong to no-one else. What a romantic scene, I thought. Just like a scene out of a tear-jerking film where the two lovers meet, we eagerly embraced each other and kissed passionately. I was aware of someone passing us on that foot-bridge, but was not bothered who saw us.

Carol smiled and said, “Are you not staying the night?”

Feeling quite puzzled by her question, I said, “Yes, of course. Why do you ask?”

“Where’s your suitcase?”

“Oh, I believe in travelling light - I’ve got everything I need.” At that time, I did not realise the significance of her question, since I had never before stayed in a hotel with anyone other than my ex-wife.

We held hands as we walked through the station and out to Carol’s car. She had a map of the area and before setting off, checked the route for Nantwich. I wished I could have helped her, but I always felt so useless in a car. Not only was I unable to drive, but I was also incapable of reading the map, road signs or names. I just hoped she did not mind me putting the responsibility on her for both navigating and driving. Carol was a good driver and I felt comfortable with her at the wheel. She had a knack of making me feel very special by, every so often, taking hold of my hand and giving it a gentle squeeze. This, together with the occasional loving glance, made me feel very contented in Carol's presence. After a while, she pulled off the road and stopped the car in a thickly wooded area. We kissed and held each other close and, after a few minutes, left the car and walked, hand in hand, through the woods. We heard, through the trees, the sound of cars being raced at high speed and headed towards the sound. As the noise became louder, a car racing circuit came into view. We watched, through a tall, metal gate, as the cars raced around the track and, after a few minutes, returned to Carol's car.

As we continued our journey through the Cheshire countryside, Carol told me more about the 'other man'. It seemed that, although she had an affair with him four years earlier, he had not felt able to marry her. Carol's own marriage had ended in divorce and, as a result, she had lived all that time with just her two children. She had still been seeing him since her divorce, for the occasional weekend. I let Carol tell me as much as she wanted without me asking her too many probing questions. I was curious, but did not feel that I should pry too much into her private life.

Nantwich was a beautiful little town, with a pleasant blend of old and new buildings. I felt a little sense of achievement when I spotted a car park where we managed to leave the car. We walked around the town centre, looking for a tourist information office but, after asking a few people, found that, by that time, it would be closed. All we wanted was to find what hotels Nantwich had to offer.

With a flash of inspiration, Carol suddenly said, "I know! Let's go into W. H. Smith's and look at the hotel guide." I thought this was a great idea and, together, soon found the bookshop. It did not take Carol long to find an 'RAC Guide to Hotels in Britain'. She leafed through the pages to find which hotels were in the area and noted the telephone numbers of a few. Of those she had noted, one looked and sounded much better than the rest and tempted us to phone it first. The hotel did have a double room available that night and with a double bed. I booked the room in my name and asked for directions.

Carol had noticed that the hotel had an indoor swimming pool and said, "It's just after five o'clock. We might just have time to buy swimming costumes before the shops close. Would you like a swim?"

"Yes, that would be great." I could not swim, but that did not matter. I would have done anything with Carol. We found a sports shop and looked through the swimwear. Carol felt that she would find something more suitable for her in the shop across the road and left me to search through the trunks. A short while later, she returned having been successful in her purchase. By that time, I had chosen a pair of trunks and asked her opinion. With her approval, I made my purchase and we then headed for the car.

About two miles outside Nantwich, we found the Rookery Hotel. It looked very impressive and was, in fact, a Georgian manor house set in large grounds. It was when we were leaving the car, that I realised my mistake. Carol had the presence of mind to bring an overnight case, which, to the hotel staff, would look more convincing and plausible than my idea of travelling light. It made me feel very inexperienced in such matters. Still, I was intent on learning fast and checked that Carol could remember my address. Since I could not fill in the register, I had to ask Carol to do this for me and register as man and wife. A thrill of excitement ran through me just at the thought of posing as a married couple. Even if the hotel receptionist did not believe us, it did not worry me in the slightest.

We walked up the wide staircase and on to a galleried balcony. Our room was off the first floor balcony and looked superb. It was large, comfortable and gave an impression of luxury. We embraced and kissed, but stopped before we became too aroused. The first thing we had to do would be to book dinner. It was fortunate that the hotel did not apply strict rules about formal dress in the restaurant, since I had stupidly not brought a change of clothes. We both stripped off and put on our swimwear, Carol seeking my approval for her choice of costume. From the short time I had known her, it was obvious that Carol had good dress sense and, on this occasion, I was not disappointed. We dressed again and went in search of the swimming pool. It was close to the tennis courts and, although not large, looked inviting.

Carol did know of my inability to swim and helped me to gain confidence in the water. Apart from us, there were only a couple of men in the pool and we were able to enjoy each other's company without feeling conspicuous. We held our bodies close in the water and kissed yet again. After about twenty minutes, we left the pool and, for the first time, separated to go and get showered and dressed in the separate changing rooms.

We returned to our room to make our appearances a little more presentable before visiting the restaurant. Our orders were taken by a smartly dressed head waiter while we had a drink in the cocktail lounge. It was a sunny, warm day and the lounge doors were open to a small courtyard where fountains of water cascaded onto stones, creating a romantic setting. We both agreed to avoid drinking too much alcohol, in case this marred our sexual activities later on. While we were sitting there, Carol asked me, once again, about my eyesight. I could never determine whether she asked out of interest or concern. My greatest fear was that she might feel unable to marry me because of my handicap. I already knew that my feelings for her were such that marriage was now one of my most sincere wishes. For this reason, I felt it important to tell her everything and to answer all questions honestly. At this time, I saw the other man as the greatest obstacle to our future happiness. I explained to Carol that, with the strong sunlight, I found it even more difficult to distinguish features clearly. When the sun is strong, my eyes feel strained and aching if I don't wear my photo chromic sun glasses. She gave my hand a squeeze of reassurance, as if to say, "Don't worry, darling. I'll stand by you."

The meal was superb, as indeed was the company. Carol always made me feel so very special, no matter what we did together. I could feel her toes against my legs, searching delicately up and down. I do not know how such a simple action could be so effective in raising my excitement, but I just hoped that this paradise would last forever. We spoon-fed each other with the starters and sweet courses, completely oblivious to other people's knowing looks. As soon as the meal was over, we returned to our room, eagerly looking forward to enjoying each other's body. Carol and I partly undressed down to our underclothes and held each other close, our mouths locked together in a deeply passionate kiss. She was wearing the sexy, black knickers I had brought her from Paris. After unfastening her bra and letting it drop to the floor, I pressed my chest against her breasts and slid my hands slowly and gently between the soft skin of her buttocks and her knickers. Slowly I eased the knickers down her thighs until they fell to the floor. Casually stepping out of them, she turned her attention to my briefs. I had purposely worn my black briefs in a probably un-necessary attempt at colour co-ordination. I do not know why, but the thought of wearing black briefs made me feel more sexy and excitable. They offered little resistance to her nimble fingers as she slid them down my legs. She was already moist as we pressed our pubic areas together. When I ran my fingers lightly up and down her buttocks, she made loud sighs of erotic pleasure and told me that she loved to feel me doing this to her. I felt her body respond to my touches as we continued to kiss and caress.

She then took hold of my hand and led me to the bathroom, where I was to experience love-making like nothing I had ever known. Carol sat on the edge of the wash-basin, with her back to the wall and facing me. While in this position, she eased herself onto my erect penis and adjusted herself until she felt comfortable. We held each other close and moved our bodies in unison until we reached a climax of erotic pleasure. Although I was envious that Carol must have had far greater sexual experience than me, I was thrilled that she knew how best to use our bodies for the maximum physical satisfaction. I wondered how many sexual partners she must have had in her life, but knew that it was none of my business and certainly not the thing to ask her. Of course, it could have only been a few, already experienced partners, which, typically, I hoped was the case. It really made me realise how sexually naive I was and, to Carol, I must have seemed like an amateur.

It did not dampen her enthusiasm, though, for she then closed the cover on the toilet seat and asked me to sit on the cover. This was yet another new experience for me as she lowered herself onto my still erect member, resting her hands on my shoulders and her buttocks on my thighs. She 'rode' me vigorously, her orgasmic sighs sounding like music to my ears. I had never known that a woman could be so vocal during love-making, but it heightened my excitement to a level I had never thought possible.

Carol again excitedly commented on how 'big' I was. Like most men, I had often wondered how I compared to other men in terms of size of organ, although I did realise that size was not the most important aspect when making love. I had heard that the average size of a British man's erect penis was between five and six inches and was quite happy that I comfortably exceeded the average.

Still, To be actually told this during love-making certainly boosted my ego. The fact that I was so gentle also seemed to give Carol an extra erotic boost. I had found that, as my eyesight deteriorated, my other senses had compensated and my sense of touch was heightened to an extent which enhanced sexual arousal for both partners.

I imagined this variety of love-making positions to be like starting a degree course in sexuality, with Carol being the experienced tutor and me the willing student. Perhaps this could be the British equivalent of the Kama Sutra. If I could achieve a first class honours degree, I may well be physically shattered, but would be very satisfied.

We next made love on the bed with Carol on top of me, for a full, deep penetration. As I looked up at her, she gave a knowing smile and kissed me with a passion so engulfing, so intense and so perfect that I felt thoroughly consumed by this captivating woman I had known for only seven weeks. At the same time, I knew that my feelings for her were not purely physical. There was a deep, emotional bond between us and I just hoped that it would last forever.

Eventually, we were both so exhausted by our energetic, yet unhurried love-making that we just lay on the bed, holding each other close. That was when I began to notice the heat. Both our bodies were burning from our exertions. Our mouths felt so dry and parched, we had to sip water to avoid discomfort. Both of us had an uncomfortable feeling of indigestion and realised that we had probably eaten too much for dinner. A new lesson I learned that night was to eat only lightly before heavy love-making. We found it impossible to sleep, either because of our discomfort or excitement and, after dawn had broken on that Sunday morning, the second day of June, we had overcome our discomfort and made beautiful love once again. Each time, there had been a lot of fore-play, a lot of touching and caressing and gentle, unhurried intercourse.

When we eventually decided to get up, we went in the shower together and soaped each other's bodies, which, though such a simple action, was extremely erotic.

We dressed and went down the broad staircase to the restaurant, where we decided not to have the full English breakfast. A lighter breakfast of scrambled eggs proved to be sufficient for our needs.

After collecting our belongings from our room, we made our way to reception to check out.

"Good morning sir, madam. Did you sleep well?"

"Oh, yes, thanks" we lied. This was probably a standard question asked of all the guests, but, in our case, we would have been foolish to say anything else, since our insomnia was self-inflicted. I signed the credit card form in my usually illegible handwriting and left the hotel to head for Carol's car. I felt a sense of sadness as I realised that, in less than an hour's time, we would have to separate. Why do the pleasurable times together seem to pass so quickly, while waiting for our next date seemed to take a lifetime?

During the journey to my house, Carol kept giving my hand an occasional squeeze of affection. I still did not know where I stood in her mind. I had been completely open and frank about my past, leaving no details out. Yet, I still knew very little about Carol other than the main events of her life. I did know that she loved me, because she kept telling me so, but the spectre of the other man still haunted what seemed to be a perfect relationship. She would not tell me even his first name, which made it awkward, having to constantly refer to him as 'the other man'. She did keep saying that she was not good enough for me and that I should find another woman. I did not want anyone else and would feel like I was cheating on her if I started seeing someone else.

When we reached my house, she said, "I can't come in, darling. I must get back for the boys." We held each other close and kissed for a few minutes while sitting in her car, and then I reluctantly opened the door and stepped into the cool morning air.

As I stepped onto the pavement, I went to her door and tapped on the window. When she wound the window down, I leaned into the car and gave her one last parting kiss. "Please drive carefully, sweetheart. Let me know when you arrive home. Bye, Carol. Love you."

"Love you, too. I'll ring as soon as I get back. Bye." I watched as her car accelerated along the road and only went indoors when I could no longer see it.

The time was just after nine thirty and, once again, I was alone in my house. I had never liked the silence, since it seemed to emphasise my isolation. The radio was my 'comforter' and, in particular, light music. As I switched the radio on, Dave Lee Travis's voice broke the silence and made the house alive again. I changed clothes and then just relaxed. I could not relax completely, though, until Carol had phoned to let me know she had returned safely. For the rest of that day, I did very little, just resting, eating and sleeping. The exertions of the previous night, combined with a lack of sleep had exhausted me. All the events of the previous twenty four hours filled my thoughts and I wondered what the future had in store for me. I knew that I had no control of the situation and that Carol was pulling all the strings. I only hoped she would love me enough to let the romance continue and, perhaps, even agree to marriage.

Late that night, the telephone rang. It was Carol. I was always pleased to hear her warm, cultured, gentle tones and she seemed to be happy. "Thanks for a wonderful time, darling. I really enjoyed being with you." Her expressions of appreciation always made me feel good. "In today's paper it says that there's a programme on television tonight called 'Everyman' which is all about a man who lost his sight and how he coped with blindness. I thought you might want to watch it."

I thanked her and said that I may watch it. We talked for a little longer and then wished each other goodnight. I did watch 'Everyman' but found the subject of the programme to be a bit self-centred and switched off after a while.

My secretary was on holiday the next day and I still felt very tired. Fortunately, there was no urgent work required that day and I spent it casually. I phoned Carol, that evening. She told me of an exhibition of aids for visually handicapped people, being held at Bristol. My heart sank as she was telling me of this exhibition. Trying to be as tactful as possible, I said, "Carol, I feel terrible at having to say this to you, but please don't think of me as a visually handicapped person. I'd sooner you thought of me as a man who loves you first and my poor eyesight last. Do you know what I mean?"

"Yes, of course, darling. I'm sorry - I was not thinking." There was a true sense of apology in her voice and I felt relieved that she was not offended.

During the next day, I had terrible pangs of conscience for rebuking Carol. I knew she was trying to help because she cared for me and I had rejected her help. Late in the evening, I phoned Carol to apologise. Unusually, it was not Carol who answered. It was her son, Peter. He said that his mum was out and had no idea what time she would be back. I had a strange feeling of apprehension as I replaced the receiver. It was unusual for her to be out so late when she was working the following day. I slept uneasily that night, wondering if anything was wrong. I did not know then but I would not have long to wait before finding out.

When I phoned Carol on Wednesday night, she sounded very subdued. In an effort to make her task a little easier, I said, "I know that sometimes you avoid saying some things to me because you know I would be hurt, but I can't be protected forever. I've a feeling I'm about to be hurt, but tell me what you want to say."

She started to cry and said in a shaky voice, "I.. I won't be able to see you again. I'm getting married."

The shock of her statement stunned me and I could not speak. Tears filled my eyes as my worst fears were realised. "I don't know what to say, Carol. I do wish you the best of luck. When are you getting married?"

"Probably in a couple of months time. I am sorry, love. Can you ever forgive me?"

"Of course I'll forgive you, but I'll never forget. Can I still phone you?" I asked nervously and hopefully.

"No, there's no point. I do love you and I always will. But there's no future for us. Please take care, darling." We were both sobbing uncontrollably as we hung up.

I was devastated. I had anticipated some bad news, but it had hit me like a sledgehammer. I was completely heart-broken and cried for what seemed like a lifetime. I went to bed, but was unable to sleep for more than an hour the whole night. Carol must have seen the other man the night before. What I could not understand was why he had changed his mind after such a long time and only two days after Carol and I had spent the night together. The conclusion I came to was that I been an unwitting catalyst in making his decision. There was a possibility that Carol had set me up to accelerate his decision, but I did not believe that she could have done that to me. It was more likely that he had realised that she was seeing someone else and knew that, if he did not do something quickly, he may lose her forever. He probably had tried to phone her while we were away and realised the truth. There was a lot of anger in me that night, but it was not directed towards Carol. I loved her more than ever, not less.

Unable to rest, I climbed out of bed around six o'clock feeling thoroughly exhausted and distressed. I had to write her a letter and switched the computer on in my office, determined to get it out of my system as soon as possible. I was in a terrible dilemma because I loved Carol so much that her happiness had to be the most important aim, while, at the same time, I felt that her loss would be unbearable. In my letter, I told her that, if she wanted me, I would have done anything to be married to her. I knew that it was now not possible and wished her future happiness. As a memento of the times we had spent together, I asked if she would let me have a photograph of her, together with a message recorded on cassette. By eight o'clock, I had posted the letter to her, hoping that what I said in it would not hurt her more.

When Kate, my secretary, arrived at nine o'clock, I must have looked terrible. She did not comment at first, but, after going through the post, she asked, "What's wrong, John?"

That was enough. I could not hold back my emotions any longer. "Carol's getting married" I blurted.

As I collapsed into tears, my statement must have taken her by surprise and she asked, disbelievingly, "What? Oh, God, no - I am so sorry." Diplomatically, she left me on my own for a few minutes while she made a drink. She helped me to get through that day and very little work was done on my part. Kate dealt with all telephone calls and protected me from having to speak to clients. I was so exhausted that I could not concentrate on anything. Carol was on my mind all of the time and everything we had said and done together kept repeating through my brain, like an endless spool of film.

Although I forced myself to do some work, the next few days were no improvement. I found it impossible to get much sleep at night and this tiredness, coupled with depression, made me feel thoroughly miserable.

I did not realise how obvious it was until Kate told me that a client asked her if I was ill. She made excuses for me by saying that I had a cold. I wanted to act normally, but found the vicious circle of tiredness and depression impossible to escape. After a week of this despair, I felt I had to do something soon. I weighed up what I had and came to the conclusion that it was not much. The business was successful, but, on its own, was not enough. Carol had affected me so much, that life without her was not worth living. Losing her had affected me far more than I could ever have imagined. Just eight days after Carol had broken the news to me of her forthcoming marriage, I felt in such a state that I could not go on any longer. I really felt that suicide was the only answer. I stayed deep in thought, for several hours trying to decide how to make the end as painless as possible. I was too much of a coward to end my life by hanging, cutting my wrist or burning myself to death and felt that an overdose of tablets would be the simplest method. At the same time, I was thinking of the consequences of my actions. Carol was already feeling guilty about abandoning our relationship and, I felt certain that taking my own life would make her feelings of guilt far, far worse. Could I do that to her?

My parents would be devastated and their health could also suffer as a result. Could I do this to them?

The answer to both these questions was an emphatic 'no'. I cared too much about all of them to finish my life. But, if I did not do that, what was I to do? There was only one other course of action. I had to phone Carol. She may not have wanted to speak to me but I had to try. What would I do if 'he' or the boys answered? Hanging up would cause suspicion and potential problems for Carol. I decided that, if this happened, I would ask for Jacquie and make it look like a genuine case of mis-dialling.

Nervously, I dialled Carol's number and, luckily, she answered in her gentle soft tones. Her voice alone was a tonic to my heart. "Hello, Carol. I know that I shouldn't, but I had to speak to you."

The tremble in her voice was noticeable as she said, "You shouldn't have phoned, but I've wanted to speak to you so much this week. I am sorry for what I've done to you, John. Are you alright?"

"I wish I could say 'Yes'. I've missed you so much, Carol. I'm exhausted from lack of sleep, I feel terrible." She clearly felt very guilty and I did not want her to feel worse, but I had to tell her the truth. "I won't phone you again, love, to avoid problems for you, but I'm hoping that you would be able to phone me, when you can. I just can't stop loving you."

She paused to choose her words carefully. "I'm not certain that it's a good idea. You know I can't phone you after my marriage."

I knew that she was being more practical than me, but, somehow, I had to convince her that she should keep in contact. "Yes, I know that, but, if I could talk to you until then, it will help me. I just can't cope with the sudden break. I've never known happiness like I've found with you and, to go from that to nothing, is too much. Do you know what I mean?"

"Yes, I understand. I will phone you when I can. I'll have to go now, but I will phone. 'Bye, love."

This was all I wanted. I wished her goodnight and, that night, slept better than I had for over a week. It was still a compromise, but a lot better than having to forget Carol completely. My thoughts of suicide were now confined to the back recesses of my mind.

Kate, my secretary, noticed an improvement in me when she came in the office that morning. When I told her of my conversation with Carol, she said, "I think you're very foolish to have phoned Carol. The best thing you could do is forget about her."

"I know it was not the most sensible thing to do, but I love her too much to just forget her."

I was pleasantly surprised when Carol phoned me that night. The fact that she had phoned so soon made me feel a little better. In my letter to her, I had asked for a photograph, but she told me that she would not send me one, since she did not feel that she came out very well on photos. I was disappointed at this, but she did promise to send me a cassette through the post. When the tape did arrive, a few days later, I listened in eager anticipation. It was short, but every word was filled with warmth, love and emotion. It made me feel good to hear her warm tones and I determined to listen to the tape, last thing at night, on the days when she did not phone.

For the next sixteen days, I heard nothing from Carol and this complete lack of contact brought back all my fears and depressions. She had asked me to go out with other women, in the hope that I would find someone else to replace her in my heart.

During those two weeks of Carol's absence, I did meet and date two women, through the introduction agency. I felt as though I was cheating on Carol in meeting anyone else, but, in fairness to her, I thought I should try and find someone else. The trouble was that my heart was tied inextricably to Carol and, no matter how desirable anyone else might have been, they could be no match to Carol. I knew that, in both cases, I was unlikely to see the woman again and felt empty and depressed after our dates.

When Carol did phone me, the following Sunday, she sounded upset. While I was on my wasted date the previous night, Carol had tried to phone me. I cursed myself for not being there when the one person I wanted to hear from, phoned. It seemed that she was missing me as much as I was missing her. Our conversation was romantic and very emotional. Much as I wished to be with her, I always slept better after just talking to her.

Four days later, she phoned again. I prayed that she would phone me at least two or three times a week. Anything beyond that would increase my feelings of anxiety and depression. If

I was to be honest, I hoped that talking to Carol again would culminate in seeing her once more. I would never give up hope as long as she continued to talk to me. I felt as though I was in a two horse race with me many lengths behind her other man and Carol as the prize. I had a lot of catching up to do but I knew that my handicap was that only Carol could control the distance between us. During our conversation, I took a chance and suggested to Carol that, once she was married, I could perhaps be her 'bit on the side'. Not surprisingly, she could not agree with this idea and said she would remain faithful to her partner unlike in her first marriage.

I had another disappointment during this traumatic month. Kate had been working for me over the past sixteen months and I was very dependent on her support. She had applied for another job in a health centre and had been accepted. I do not know if the situation with Carol had made her feel insecure about her future prospects working for me, but it came as a shock when she told me of her plans to leave the company in August. She did assist me in finding a replacement and helped to interview several potential ladies for the post. Birgit was a very pleasant German woman who, I felt certain, would be a capable and competent secretary. She was very professional and spoke excellent English with only a hint of a German accent.

CHAPTER FOUR - JULY, 1991

At the end of each conversation, Carol usually told me when she thought she could ring again. I was surprised to receive an unexpected call only two days later. She was in tears and sobbed that she was missing me more than she could bear. While her need for me boosted my ego, I was concerned for her own state of mind. The fact that she was only a month away from her forthcoming marriage, and still very much in love with me, must have caused her such emotional torment that she could not possibly have any peace of mind. I felt certain that she was having doubts about marrying the other man, but I did not know whether it was because of me or other factors. I must admit that I was curious to know more about the full situation, but also knew that I had no right to expect Carol to tell me everything.

There was so much more that I wanted to know about Carol, but did not dare to ask. She would tell me all that I needed to know at any one time. Over the period I had known her, I had told her everything about my life, mainly because I did not want to have any secrets from the woman I loved and I hoped that, in time, she would feel the same about me.

Late the following evening, Carol phoned yet again. She always wanted to know what I had been doing and showed a high level of interest in me. Talking to her was so easy and natural, that our conversations could often last for well over an hour, without realising it. Two days later, on a Tuesday evening, the phone rang. By this time, I knew if the phone rang after ten thirty, that it could only be Carol and would answer simply, "Carol, darling." For twenty or thirty minutes, we would mix conversation of a general nature with intimate expressions of our love.

Again the following evening, she phoned just after ten thirty. We talked for a while and then wished each other goodnight. I was yet to discover this night was to be different from all the others. At eleven thirty, she rang me again. She was in bed and very tired, but wished I could have been with her. I would have given anything in the world to be in her bed, but I knew that she was expressing a desire and not an actual request. Until she did, I would continue to enjoy our telephonic romance.

What I could not understand, was why she was obviously speaking to me the last thing before falling asleep, instead of talking to the man she was due to marry. She seemed to be using my voice as a 'comforter' in the same way a child would use a teddy bear. Quite often, after these late night romantic conversations, I would be sexually aroused and feel frustrated that we could not be locked together in ecstatic love-making.

Over the next weeks, she phoned me practically every night and continued our secret relationship. I was certain that her children knew nothing of our friendship and, in fact, she had told me that nobody knew about us. I felt it was a pity that she did not have a friend in whom she could confide and seek advice. One evening, she said that she loved talking to me because I was an 'outsider' and could help her by listening to all her problems. It was then that I realised I was the close friend I thought she needed. The trouble was that the last thing I wanted to be was an 'outsider'. She did tell me that she was not now getting married as soon as she had initially anticipated.

Up until the last week in July, we talked on the phone practically every night of the week. On some occasions, I would ask her to let me see her, but, in all cases, she refused. I felt certain that she wanted to be with me, but did not want to create complications in her relationship with the other man. I did not hear from her at the end of that month as she took her children on holiday. During those days without hearing her voice on the telephone, I would play the cassette she had recorded, last thing at night before going to sleep. The roles had now been reversed and I was using her recorded voice as my 'comforter'. The greatest comfort of all would have been to hear her say 'Yes' to my proposal of marriage. At that time, it seemed an impossible dream and I was living from day to day with the thought of Carol uppermost in my mind. Nothing else seemed to have any relevance at all and, since Carol had broken the news of her impending marriage to me almost two months earlier, I had slept badly. I was constantly tired and found great difficulty in concentrating on anything, including my work.

She did phone shortly after returning from holiday and the sound of her voice excited me once again. I thought I would take a chance and asked if I could see her again. Once more, she refused to allow such a meeting, much to my dismay. I felt certain that she wanted me, but was strong willed enough to resist the temptation. My will-power, on the other hand, was non-existent where Carol was concerned. I do have a strong sense of self-discipline in all other respects, but I would have given everything else up just to be with Carol.

On a few occasions, Carol did say that, if we were to marry, she did not feel able to give me the support she thought I would need as my eyesight became worse. I did try to assure her that it need not place many demands on her, since I would have to adapt to a changing situation. To my mind, she would be perfectly capable of giving me all the moral support I might need. If the situation was reversed, I knew that I would do absolutely everything possible for her, no matter what the handicap.

Only a day later, she phoned and was upset. Tearfully, she told me that she was feeling very low, but did not know why. Since she told me very little about the other man, I did not know whether he or I was the source of the problem. To my great surprise, she did agree, at last, that we should meet. My spirits were immediately uplifted and I wondered how soon we could see each other.

I had not told Carol, but my eyesight was a great source of

concern and despair to me. I knew that, over a period of time, it would get worse, but since changes were very gradual, it was difficult to monitor. I was depressed at the realisation that, although I had recently become suntanned, I could not see the freckles on my arms, even though I had been told that they were there. To most people, it would have appeared to be an insignificant fact, but, to me, it represented yet another loss in my troubled life.

When Carol phoned, the next day, I was stunned when she told me that her other man was not yet divorced. I had mistakenly believed that his marriage had ended within the last few months. It was little surprise, therefore, that her marriage plans had been delayed. It also indicated, to me, that this man was not sufficiently committed to Carol to end his marriage and, clearly, did not deserve her love. I also wondered what his wife thought of Carol, the woman who had an affair with her husband? Was she, perhaps, trying to save their marriage and, in the process, spoiling Carol's own marriage plans?

CHAPTER FIVE - AUGUST, 1991

The first day of August saw another development in our relationship which uplifted my spirits. That was the first day on which Carol allowed me to telephone her again. It would have to be late in the evening when the children were in bed. Carol was in bed herself when I phoned and we had a good conversation in which we arranged a date to see each other.

I had booked into a hotel on the outskirts of Chester and, although she would not be able to stay overnight, Carol would have dinner with me and stay as late as she could. There was still a week before our meeting and many doubts filled Carol's mind about the sense of our re-union. My fears were heightened even more when she told me that, in those few days, she would be taking the children away and they would all be staying with her other man. I wondered why his ever-tolerant wife would allow such a situation? I felt envious that he would be spending so much time with the woman I loved. I prayed that their time together would not deter her from our secret rendezvous.

I was very relieved when Carol phoned me a day before our meeting and arranged a suitable time. On the Friday night, I left my office early and travelled by train to Chester. When the taxi pulled up outside the impressive entrance to the Crabwall Manor hotel, I realised that I had picked a place of real quality. Everything about the hotel exuded luxury, from the huge bedroom to the beautiful gardens and grounds. The complimentary bowl of fresh fruit and small decanter of sherry set this hotel apart from any other in which I had stayed. I asked for a porter to show me round the hotel, since it seemed a complicated layout. He was very patient as I traced my steps from the bedroom to the cocktail lounge and to the restaurant. I wanted to memorise the route to prevent me from appearing foolish when Carol was with me.

I showered, shaved and dressed for dinner and realised that I was just as nervous about seeing Carol as I was on our first date. It was ten weeks since I had last seen her, ten very long, traumatic weeks. How could one woman have given me more joy than I had ever known and yet be the cause of so much pain and anguish?

At seven fifteen, I was in the cocktail lounge waiting for Carol to appear. After only a few minutes, she walked in and I felt so pleased to see her again. We hugged and kissed, more politely than passionately, in view of the surroundings. I ordered a drink for Carol. She chose a dry Martini and, noticing my drink, asked what I was having.

"Oh, that's orange juice. I thought I should avoid having too much alcohol - I don't want it to affect my performance." I gave her a knowing smile.

"Of course - I should have done the same. I'm sorry, love." She affectionately squeezed my hand and, with this simple action, revived all the memories of the times we had spent together.

The head waiter took our orders and we did not have long to wait before our table was ready. The meal was, undoubtedly, one of the best I had ever eaten. The company of the woman I had longed to see, the good food, a bottle of wine, the romantic setting all helped to make it a wonderful, memorable evening. A special touch was added by a woman pianist, playing a suitably romantic selection of tunes. I was appreciative of the fact that, without Carol, everything else would have been meaningless.

I did notice, as the meal progressed, that Carol was becoming more intoxicated. It was Carol who spilled the coffee and not me as one might expect. What I had not realised was that, before meeting me, she had shared a bottle of wine with a neighbour. It was of little surprise, therefore, that she left the restaurant with me after the meal, asking me to look after her, guiding her in the right direction. Carol thought the bedroom was fantastic and enthused about the various touches of luxury in the room. It was the first time, that night, that we had been alone together and we made the most of it by holding each other close and kissing with an energetic passion. Ten long weeks of separation had made the strength of the reunion that much greater and we hurriedly undressed to enjoy the close contact of skin on skin.

Our love-making was energetic and Carol seemed to be charged with a wildness that heightened my excitement and pleasure beyond imagination. "Darling, I love you so much" she said many times as our love-making became more frenetic. It was re-assuring to hear her declarations, but what she did say next surprised me. "Darling, I don't want you to make love with any other woman. I'll satisfy all your needs."

The words were like music to my ears. To give such a promise, she must have decided to make our relationship more permanent. This was just what I wanted and I readily agreed not to see anyone else. It was shortly after that, when Carol began to feel unwell. The effects of the evening's drinks had caught up with her and meant that our passionate activities had to cease.

We both dressed and, after making certain that she was alright, I walked with her down to the hotel car park.

"Are you sure you're fit to drive?" I asked anxiously. She assured me she was and promised to drive carefully.

"I'll phone you, darling" were her last words as her car disappeared down the long hotel drive.

When I pressed the button on my talking watch, it announced, "It's eleven forty five p.m." I walked slowly and thoughtfully back to my bedroom, wishing that she could have stayed for the night. We had been together for only four and a half hours. Four and a half hours after a ten week gap. I knew that I should be grateful that she had seen me at all and, yet, her declarations less than an hour earlier gave me great hope for our future relationship. For her to promise to satisfy all my sexual needs, her strength of feelings towards me must have been very secure. I just hoped she could keep her promise.

The next morning, Carol telephoned and apologised for having too much to drink while she was with me. She was feeling better and, to my surprise, said she would come and see me again at about eleven that morning. Much cheered by this news, I waited eagerly to see her again. My hopes were soon dashed, however, when I received another telephone call. It was Carol and she was calling from a phone box. She had become stuck in a traffic jam and, because she could not have stayed long, felt that she would not be able to see me at the hotel. She asked what time I would be back from my visit to Chester city centre and promised to telephone shortly after I returned. I took a taxi into Chester just after midday and spent the next four hours exploring the city. I did walk round the wall but it did not seem the same as when Carol was with me. I did enjoy the street musicians and liked the lively atmosphere of the city centre.

It was nearly five o'clock when I returned to my hotel and hurried to my room to await Carol's call. I felt really depressed when she told me that she had actually called at the hotel around four thirty. To miss her by thirty minutes was too much and my mind was only eased when she said she would join me for breakfast the next morning, the day of my birthday. The idea appealed to me and, if I could see her again, any time together would be treated as a very special occasion.

I spent a relaxing evening, starting with a superb meal and ending in the lounge, listening to the live piano music and talking for a while to the woman pianist.

At around eight thirty, the next morning, the phone in my room rang. I knew it could only be Carol. "Happy birthday, darling. I'm sorry, but I'm not going to be able to come to see you, this morning." My heart sank at this depressing news. "I'm not feeling very well and I've had a bad night. I feel so tired. I'm so sorry, darling."

"Don't worry, love. You can't help being ill. Have a good

rest today, and I'll phone you late tonight, when I get home." I was much more disappointed than my voice indicated. I knew that she could not help being ill, but to be cheated out of seeing her three times in two days was just too much to bear. My breakfast, although good, did not raise my spirits in any way and I spent the morning doing nothing much at all. The only leisure activity in the hotel was a snooker table and, although I had not played the game for over twenty years, I was determined to try my hand before leaving the hotel. It was a good, full size table and I felt that I would be satisfied if I could pot a few balls. It was much harder than I had imagined, since I could not actually see the pockets clearly on the far side of the balls. After a little practise, I did actually manage to pot a few and felt satisfied with my performance. Even so, I was relieved that there were no spectators judging my meagre efforts.

I arrived back home at about one thirty and, once again, entered the world of loneliness. I did have to admit that this loneliness had become portable. As long as I was separated from Carol, I would feel isolated, no matter how many people surrounded me. I wondered if I would ever have Carol to myself. All I could do was hope that she would, in time, transfer her affections from the other man to me.

We phoned each other fairly regularly over the next few days until, once again, we were interrupted by Carol taking her children on holiday. When she returned, I asked her when we could meet again. She replied, "I don't know. Please don't pressure me. I feel guilty when you ask something of me which I can't do."

I had previously realised that, when she started talking this way, I had no option but to back down. Why, oh why, did not she need me as much as I needed her? I knew that I was letting her dominate the relationship, but I felt that, if I wanted it to continue at all, I had no alternative.

After thinking carefully about what she had said, I told her when we next spoke that I would not call her again, but would still love to hear from her whenever she wanted to call me. I knew that, by doing this, I stood a chance of not hearing from her again, but I just hoped that would not be the case.

For a few days, I spent an anxious, depressing time without hearing Carol's voice, but, eventually, was relieved to receive a call from her. Our conversations were always happy, natural and relaxed no matter what we talked about. I felt even better when she said that I could phone her whenever I wanted. I wondered what had changed her mind, but, as long as she would talk to me, I did not care. I was later to discover that she and her other man were having a difficult time and had agreed not to see each other for a while. I took good advantage of her concession and began phoning her more and more frequently until it became a daily occurrence.

CHAPTER SIX - SEPTEMBER, 1991

As far as I knew, Carol had kept our friendship a secret from her family and friends, presumably to protect her relationship with the other man. It came as a great surprise, therefore, when she said I could send her a card for her forty-fifth birthday on the fifteenth of September. The only condition was that it should not be too affectionate and expressive. This was a great achievement and I felt at last that I had been accepted.

Better still, she also said she would meet me one evening in September. She would have dinner and stay as late as possible, though she would not be able to stay overnight. After such a long time without seeing her, this came as a tremendous relief and a welcome excitement. I booked a room for myself, again at the Crabwall Manor hotel, just outside Chester, where I had stayed in August. A table for two was also booked for, what I hoped, would be a wonderful dinner.

The biggest surprise, however, came when Carol asked me, ten days before our date, if I could find a hotel where we could stay together for a couple of nights. This was to be on the weekend before our previously arranged date, which did not give me much time to organise. To be asked to stay with Carol for the weekend made me feel like a small boy who had just been told that he was going to see Santa at a city-centre store. I was so thrilled by the proposition that I had difficulty thinking of anything else. After a few phone calls, I found that the hotel in Nantwich, The Rookery, where we had stayed during May, was the best choice.

When I called her back with the details, she seemed happy at my arrangements and we agreed to meet at Northwich.

That Friday afternoon, I travelled by train to Northwich, arriving a little earlier than expected. I waited in eager anticipation in the station's waiting room and, after a short while, saw Carol enter the room. I could not be certain that it was Carol from that distance, but her soft, warm voice soon removed any doubts. We kissed and hugged, then walked, hand in hand, to her car.

She had told her family and friends that she was going on a course and she authenticated this by bringing a computer with her. My official role was to assist her in learning some new software necessary for her school lectures. I felt certain the hotel staff were surprised to see us carrying a complete BBC computer system into the bedroom. This time, unlike our first "dirty weekend" together, I did take a small suitcase with me. We spent so much time in our room that the chambermaid had to change the bed and clean the room around us.

For the next forty three hours, we hardly left each other's side. We walked in the sunny, but breezy September air along the Cheshire lanes, enjoying just being together. On the Saturday, we went into the centre of Nantwich and found an Antiques Fair where we stayed for a little while. Although there was a wide selection of antiques, we found nothing of interest to purchase. Back at the hotel, a great deal of the time was spent in our bedroom, alternating between using the computer and making wild, beautiful love. Carol was again in a passionate, erotic mood and the energetic thrusts of our bodies exhausted me on occasions. I did not mind since I would put up with anything to be intimate with her. I felt so comfortable in her presence and just wished that this weekend could last forever. Carol was embarrassed to discover during energetic sexual intercourse that her menstruation had started, resulting in the bed sheets becoming soiled. The chambermaid was very understanding and quickly changed the sheets for us, without complaint or comment. This did not deter us from further intercourse, but we were more careful.

On Sunday, we checked out of the hotel and drove towards Northwich. There was plenty of time before my train allowing us more chance to travel leisurely, stopping at Davenham for a drink and snack. By one fifteen, we were sitting on a platform seat at Northwich station. I knew this weekend of bliss was shortly to end and regretted that it ever had to. Carol was surprised how soon I heard the train as it approached the station, but I knew that my hearing was better than average. I gave her one last, parting kiss as the train pulled into the station.

After boarding, I waved to Carol as the train slowly accelerated in the direction of Manchester. I knew that my love for Carol was complete and inescapable, as I felt that part of me was missing as soon as we were separated. When I arrived home, it seemed so quiet and devoid of life that my loneliness returned once more. How much longer would I have to wait for the woman I loved to share my life?

Over the next few days, I spoke to Carol daily and felt relieved that I would be seeing her again, on Friday evening. I just prayed that she would not cancel our date. During the five months I had known Carol, I had realised that she did have a tendency towards indecision and yet she was prone to acting on sudden impulse. In some ways, these traits added to her attraction, as she contrasted so much with my ex-wife whose ways were so regimented that everything was far too predictable and organised.

To my relief, the arrangements were left unchanged and, on Friday, I travelled to Chester, a journey which was now becoming very familiar. It was my second visit to Crabwall Manor hotel and the room was again superb and very luxurious. I unpacked and then freshened up ready to meet the one woman in the world I wanted to be with.

At seven fifteen, I walked into the cocktail lounge, ordered chilled orange juice and sat waiting for Carol. I still felt a little anxious in case something went wrong to spoil the evening. After only a few minutes, Carol entered and sat next to me. We kissed and hugged and, once again, I felt elated in her presence. How could one woman be so utterly captivating?

When our table was ready, we walked through to the restaurant and took our places at a candle-lit table. Carol seemed to be very happy and we both enjoyed our meal. As usual, we shared our meals and occasionally spoon-fed each other.

While we were eating our main course, with romantic piano music playing in the background, I looked into Carol's eyes and said, "Carol, darling, I love you so much. Will you marry me?"

I knew this question could anger her as she had said, on many occasions, that I should find someone else who could be better for me. The truth was that I could not love anybody else as I loved Carol. Nothing less than marriage would satisfy my desires. I still did not know how Carol's relationship with her other man was at that time, but I felt that I must ask for her hand in marriage.

She gulped on her drink a little, took hold of my hand and asked, "You still want to marry me after all I've done to you?"

"More than ever, I know that I want to marry you. It would make me the happiest man alive."

Then, more than at any other time, I wished that I could see well enough to make out her expression. Was she thinking seriously about marrying me? Or, was she thinking of the most suitable way of rejecting me, without hurting my feelings too much?

She chose her words carefully and spoke in a concerned tone. "John, Darling. I wish you hadn't asked me. I do love you, but I can't marry you. My heart is not free as long as I still love someone else. I'm sorry, love, I just can't marry you."

I tried to put a brave face on, but, unfortunately, I am not very good at concealing my feelings. I felt a mixture of anger and frustration. I was being denied the woman I loved by some fool who really did not deserve her affection. "Okay, I'm sorry I asked. I suppose I knew what the answer would be. I won't ask again."

She gave me a comforting smile, squeezed my hand and said, "Let's just enjoy each other as much as possible without adding any complications. I do love this hotel. We'll finish our coffee and then go to your room."

When Carol saw the room, she thought it was wonderful. Every room in the hotel was a different design and, at that time, it was the most luxurious place I had stayed at in Britain. She pulled the cords to close the curtains and then came up to me and held me close. Our lips melted together in a fusion of passion and we began to slowly strip each other naked. She loved me to suck her breasts and, as soon as her proud, erect nipples were exposed, I placed my lips around each one in turn and sucked. This gave her such an erotic sensation that she almost squealed with delight. We did not say anything as our excitement increased. No words were necessary. Our breathing became louder and faster as we pressed our hot, naked bodies close. I lay back on the bed and pulled her down onto me. She was very moist as she straddled my body and rode me vigorously. The noise of her loud, orgasmic sighs always made my erection even bigger and stronger.

Making love with Carol was an experience I could never have imagined before I met her. There was an exhilarating wildness about her when she became really excited. That night she seemed to be even more passionate than usual and, after reaching our orgasmic pinnacles together, we collapsed exhausted. We still held each other tight, kissed tenderly and felt our hearts pounding against each other.

After a while, she looked at the time and said, "I'm going to have to leave you, now. I must go and collect the children. Do you mind if I phone them?"

"Not at all, help yourself." Her two children were staying at her ex-husband's for the evening. I wondered as she spoke to them just what they thought she was doing. I had asked her once what she told the children and she replied that she would prefer not to say. This obviously meant that she was deceiving them about her excursions. I wondered if they believed her. As she started to dress, I pulled on some clothes. I knew that she would feel uncomfortable slipping past reception on her own, so

I walked out to the car park with her. We gave each other a long, parting kiss before Carol took her place in the driving seat of her car. "Phone me when you get home, then I'll know that you've arrived safely."

"I will, darling. Love you." She drove out of the car park and down the hotel's long drive. I walked back to my room with a heavy heart. The one uncertainty with Carol was that I never knew when I would be able to see her again, if at all. I was now becoming accustomed to her swings of affection and hoped eventually to be assured of her lasting love. I felt certain that it was just a matter of time before she would accept me on a more permanent basis.

Saturday, the following day, was spent very leisurely. I stayed in bed quite late and then asked at reception if I could see the manager of the hotel. A very smartly dressed man introduced himself to me. I asked if it would be possible to see some of the other rooms at the hotel. He was very pleased to do this and escorted me around the historic building, showing me the many different suites which were available. Although I could not see any fine detail, I was able to get a good impression of the feel and quality of the rooms. In one room, there was even a huge, four-poster bed. I had always wanted to sleep in one of these and hoped that Carol and I would be able to stay for a night in that particular suite. I imagined us making passionate love together in this huge, medieval bed.

Later, I took a taxi drive to Chester and spent a couple of hours wandering around the shops. Shopping, when on my own, was now no longer a pleasure, since I could not even tell what was in the shop windows. It looked to be just a blur of different colours and, usually, nothing distinctive to even indicate what type of shop I was looking into. Still, I was determined to live as normal a life as possible and did not want to succumb to my handicap by staying indoors all the time.

The evening meal was superb and, after eating my fill, I went into the lounge area and sat near to Pat, the pianist, listening to the pleasant, relaxing music. When she had her break, I offered her a drink and stayed chatting with her for a while. She happily played a few requests for me, including 'Every time I say goodbye'. I felt that this tune was particularly appropriate for the 'on and off' romance between Carol and me. Even though I had not seen her that day, I had spoken to Carol on the phone at least three times.

The following day, I again spent a leisurely morning and returned home early afternoon. Once again, I was brought back from heaven and down to earth with the return to everyday domestic duties. This week, though, was to prove to be a little different.

CHAPTER SEVEN - OCTOBER, 1991

When I was in my mid-thirties, I had undergone a double hernia repair and had recently experienced some pain in my right groin when lifting heavy objects or when standing for any length of time. As a consequence, I had seen a consultant and he felt it wise to operate again to relieve the pain. An advantage of using private health care is the ability to schedule the operation to suit my circumstances and booked into the Alexandra private hospital for the first week in October.

I had not told anybody except my secretary and Carol about the operation, since I felt my parents would worry unnecessarily. I would tell them about the operation when I next saw them. Carol disappointed me when she said she could not visit me in hospital. I could not understand why, but I did know that she did not like illness in anyone close to her and avoided situations where she was directly faced with it. I knew this was one of her less attractive features, as true love should be able to withstand any times when one was victim to illness or disease. For my part, I knew that I would want to care for her no matter what was wrong.

I had taken my Kurzweil Personal Reader into hospital with me and this caused quite a bit of interest amongst the nursing staff. This device allowed me to scan a printed document using a small, hand held camera and its contents would then be read back to me by a very intelligible speech synthesiser with a pleasant,

American accent. I had some computer manuals with me and would read them using this device if I felt fit enough.

On the evening before my operation, the telephone in my room rang and I was pleased to hear Carol's soft, reassuring tones. I know that I slept better for having spoken to her. Hernia operations are fairly minor, these days and mine was no exception, though I always felt that any operation requiring a general anaesthetic was potentially risky. The nurses at the hospital were really good and, whenever they had a spare moment, would come and talk to me when they realised that I did not have any visitors. Carol did telephone me every day, but it was my secretary, Birgit, who collected me from the hospital and brought me home.

The telephone conversations with Carol were now a regular daily feature and it seemed to be the perfect end to the day to lie in bed talking to the woman I loved. Even though many of our calls lasted for more than an hour, we were never short of things to say. She did admit that she had neither seen nor spoken to the other man for at least two months. Carol did not feel that her relationship with him could ever work, but, equally, she did not feel that marriage to me would ever be possible.

The reason she gave for this was that, although she felt that she did love me, it was not the 'deep love' feeling she had experienced with the other man. This chemical attraction, she was certain, should be something that is felt within minutes of meeting and so, until she had this feeling again, she would not marry. I was certain that this was an idealistic viewpoint and that a good marriage is based on long-standing trust, honesty and affection.

Over a period of time, Carol told me more and more about the other man. Apparently, she had always adopted a cheerful attitude in his presence, no matter how badly she felt. This was because he could not stand to see her sad and had, instead, preferred her to disguise any feelings of depression. I felt this to be a completely unrealistic and selfish attitude and told her so. She knew with me that she could be completely open and honest and I would listen and talk to her no matter how low or upset she may feel.

One of Carol's worst characteristics was changeability. During one evening's telephone conversation, she would say how much she still loved the other man and did not feel right about me, while she would phone me in the middle of the next night and tell me how she really loved me. It was a very confusing time, during which my insecurity fluctuated according to her mood.

Carol had arranged to go to her sister's for a week's holiday during mid October and, before leaving, I asked her to telephone me whenever possible. Since she did not want her sister to know of my existence, I knew it would be difficult for her to call me. She said she would, but I was again disappointed by the complete silence from her. I felt certain that, if she really loved me and was thinking about me, she would find a way to call.

CHAPTER EIGHT - NOVEMBER, 1991

At the beginning of November, Carol's best friend, Barbara, had invited her to a dance on a Saturday evening. Barbara would be with her husband, and this made Carol feel that she would be the odd one out. I felt the solution was obvious and offered to be her partner. It came as no surprise when she rejected the offer, since it would ruin her idea of keeping my existence a secret. In the event, she did not go to the dance and spent at least two hours talking to me on the phone. How I wished I could travel along that telephone wire and be with her, holding her tight in her bed.

To my surprise, on the following day, a Sunday, she telephoned me mid morning and asked if she could come and see me for a few hours. I would have been a fool to refuse, since I had not seen her for five weeks and was desperate to hold her again. Shortly after mid day, she arrived at my house. I hugged and kissed her as though we had been separated for years. The main reason for her visit was that she was feeling very low and could not stand being on her own.

Carol did not want to stay in the house and so we drove into the Cheshire countryside. It was a cold, wet November day. Not a day to get much pleasure from driving along narrow country lanes littered with large pools of water. Dunham Park provided temporary shelter for about twenty minutes as we wandered around the buildings where many people had gathered. Stalls had been set up where garden and indoor plants were on display. Carol did buy a plant, but we realised that there was not much else to see, so we rushed back to the car in the pouring rain.

By this time, we were both feeling quite hungry, giving us a good excuse to stopped at a pub where we had a meal. I did notice that Carol was a little more distant than usual, but put this down to her depression. She did seem pleased when we found an Antiques Fair at a hotel and spent quite a while looking at the many tables covered with plates, dishes and many other items, some of which, we were certain, did not qualify as antiques.

When we did eventually arrive back at my house, I was perceptive enough to realise that she was not in a sexually excitable mood. Even though we had not made love for five weeks, I knew that I was going to have to wait until we could meet again. I remembered her promise to always keep me sexually satisfied, but thought better of mentioning it. We talked for a little while until late afternoon, when Carol had to return home to make a meal for the children.

That night, when we talked on the telephone, we tried to determine the cause of her depression. She admitted to a feeling of deep humiliation that the other man seemed to have abandoned her. To my mind, he must never have loved her properly if he could not go through with marrying her. After a lengthy discussion, she felt a little comforted by my reassurances and began to feel drowsy. On many occasions, Carol would actually fall asleep while holding the phone. My voice seemed to soothe her troubled mind to a surprising degree. When this happened, I would say in a whisper which she could hear without waking fully, "Carol, darling. Put the receiver down and have a lovely sleep. Goodnight, love." She would obediently follow my instruction and, in a very sleepy voice reply, "Bye, John. Love you."

It struck me as strange that I should be used as a counsellor for Carol's relationship with her previous lover. I did not mind as long as I was able to be emotionally close to her. My own sleep was disturbed the following morning by Carol telephoning me because she was, once again, depressed and upset at her situation. We could not talk for long as we both had to get ready for work, but I managed to calm her down once more. On that day, we spoke to each other on three occasions, since Carol phoned me early evening and I phoned her last thing at night as usual. Although I would obviously prefer to actually be with Carol, I was pleased that we had so much contact, but, more than anything else, it boosted my self-confidence that someone I cared for actually wanted me and relied upon my help to get them through the day.

This pattern of talking to each other first thing in the morning and last thing at night was repeated for every day that week. Towards the end of the week, when she was feeling low, she said, "This horrible cold weather gets me down. There's just nothing to look forward to. I wish I could go somewhere warm."

I knew that, over Christmas, Carol and the children would be going to her sister's, but that certainly would not be warm. I had a sudden idea and said, "Carol, when is your half-term holiday?"

"Late next February, but I'm not certain of the dates. Why?"

"Let's go away together, during half-term, to somewhere really warm," I suggested. "How about Florida?"

"Oh, John, that would be lovely. It doesn't have to be Florida, you know. As long as it's warm and restful. Do you think we can?"

"Of course. If that's what you would like, I'd love to take you."

"What about the children? My ex-husband might not have them during that week."

"That's no problem." I replied, confidently. "If he won't look after them, we'll just take them with us. You know that I don't mind." She accepted this and seemed so happy at the idea, that her spirits were lifted and the rest of her conversation had a much more optimistic tone. She soon became drowsy and fell asleep. I could sleep soundly now that I had comforted her.

I was hoping to see Carol on the Saturday, but she phoned to tell me that she could not come, since she had to look after the children that night. Once again, I was disappointed. If only she would let me stay at her house, it would have solved so many problems. She told me so many times that she did not like sleeping alone and, yet, she would not let me openly and without shame into her life to keep her company. I found it so difficult to understand.

Even though we did not see each other much at that time, we talked for more time on the phone than most husbands and wives would talk when they lived together. One of our evening telephone calls lasted for an hour and a half. We would talk together last thing every night and first thing every morning. I noticed that, on many occasions, I was physically aroused just talking to her.

It was about the middle of November that I learned of the name of Carol's other man. He was called Dave Thomas and she had, apparently, met him in the course of her job. After the break-up of Carol's marriage, both she and Dave changed jobs, presumably to avoid too much scandal.

Carol did agree to let me take her to the theatre during November. She arrived at my house on a Saturday evening and, as soon as I saw her, I went to give her a big hug and a kiss. It was obvious, though, that something was wrong. She let me hug her, but would not put her arms around me. That night, she seemed unusually reserved and distant.

Alan Ayckbourne's play, 'Man of the Moment' at the Forum Theatre in Wythenshawe was excellent and we both enjoyed it. Unfortunately, Carol gave the impression that she would have preferred to be somewhere else or, worse still, with someone else. I just hoped that it was more of an indication of hormonal stress related to her menstrual cycle. Understandably, she did not want to make love that night. Even though I, once again, felt insecure about our relationship and slept badly that night, Carol still phoned me early next morning. At times, I had the feeling that she would be happier just to have telephone contact.

Early in November, I did something which I had never thought possible before. Since my eyesight was not good enough for me to drive, I had no choice but to use public transport for getting around. This had always been a major limitation to mobility. I had formed my own computer company in nineteen seventy eight and was now tiring of relying on the poor service provided by British Rail and local bus services. I had made my mind up to buy myself a car. I knew that, for office use, my secretary could drive me wherever I needed to go and I hoped that Carol would also use it when we had to go anywhere at weekends.

I was hoping that Carol would help me to choose a suitable car, but it was actually my secretary, Birgit, who drove me round the various garages. Both of us instantly fell in love with the bright red SAAB 900i as soon as we spotted it on the forecourt of Andersons, a Stockport garage. When I told Carol of my purchase, she seemed to be really pleased, especially when I told her that she would be able to drive it on the insurance cover I had taken out.

My son, who I did not see very often, called round on a Sunday afternoon and saw the gleaming car in my drive. I had just let him in the house and was telling him about the car, when the phone rang. I excused myself, went into the other room and answered the phone. As I had expected, it was Carol. She was in a terrible state and sobbing uncontrollably. I could not leave her in that state and spent several minutes trying to comfort her. She was always convincing herself that she had no future and that she would never meet the man who would be the person to marry. Unfortunately, I did not seem to count, much to my dismay. When she was feeling better, I told her of my son's visit and said I would ring back as soon as he had left. My son knew nothing of my female relationships since my separation and he did not ask who the caller had been. My thoughts were still with Carol as I proudly showed off the beautifully engineered Swedish car. He was both surprised and impressed that I had chosen such a car.

When I did phone Carol back, she seemed quite composed, but it was not until our bedtime conversation that she, once again, hurt me by what she said. After our dates where she had driven the fifty miles to my house, she always had a long, lonely drive home. This had been getting her down and she felt that she did not want to do it again. We had arranged to meet at the end of November and that was now unlikely. She was even having second thoughts about my suggestion of the Florida holiday in February. Why did she have to destroy every good thing between us? I could have understood it if it was only for my benefit, but that was not the case.

Carol had, on many occasions, suggested that I should see another woman. Although I knew where my heart lay, I arranged to take another woman to see 'Kiss me Kate' at the Opera House. It seemed strange to be with someone other than Carol for the evening. Although we seemed to get on alright with each other, we did not arrange to meet again. I did not know whether she could tell that my heart was reserved for someone else or if she was not attracted towards me. It did not really bother me.

I had told Carol of my date and, when I telephoned her late that night, she showed interest in the other woman. There even seemed to be, so I thought, a hint of jealousy in her questions. If anything, I felt that the evening had strengthened our relationship.

When Carol and I had stayed in the Rookery Hotel at Nantwich during May, I had felt ashamed of myself for not being able to swim. As a consequence, I had determined to learn how to overcome my fear of water. My chance came, when my secretary spotted an advert in a private health magazine for a swimming school. It seemed a good idea and, after a few phone calls during August, I had booked myself on a course starting on 22nd. November. I told nobody except my secretary. The only fact I had told Carol, was that I was going away for a week's course, but did not tell her what I was studying. She was curious, but accepted that she would find out at the end of the week when I wanted to meet her.

My main concern was that she may need to contact me urgently if she had a period of severe depression. I thought how I could be available to help her, should this occur, without giving my location away. The solution was to write a letter to Carol and enclose the telephone number of the school in a sealed envelope. I gave her instructions in my letter that she was only to open the envelope if she desperately needed to call me. I also intended to phone her whenever I could.

I felt very nervous about the events of the coming week as I took the lengthy train journey from Manchester Piccadilly station. The fact that the engine had to be replaced twice, on the five hour journey to Exeter, reinforced my opinions of British Rail and I was thankful that I no longer needed to rely on them for local travel. A taxi took me the last few miles to the Long Range Swimming School, which was a strange, rambling place. It seemed to be a large, country house which had been extended and altered so much that it no longer resembled the original building. The quality of the hotels I had stayed in over the past two years had spoiled me and left me feeling very dissatisfied with my room. It was a double one, since that was all that was left for this week, but it was so cramped that I wondered what on earth the single rooms were like. It was so small that, if I wanted to open my wardrobe, I had to move the chair behind the door. There was a telephone, but I had to climb over the bed to get to it and the television did not work. Still, the purpose of the week was to learn to swim and I could not be too fussy about the accommodation.

I joined the other students for the evening meal and had a few drinks in the bar, making polite conversation with my fellow victims. Nobody stayed up late for that first night and I went to my room just before eleven. I undressed, slipped into bed and picked up the telephone receiver to call Carol. To my dismay, I was unable to get a dialling tone. No matter what I did, the phone would not work. I dialled my own home number and had a similar lack of success. My frustration increased as I discovered that the reception staff finished at ten thirty. I sat on the bed, wondering what on earth I could do. Carol would be waiting for my call and I was not going to let her down.

With a sudden inspiration, I pulled on my track suit and left my room. I crept silently down the stairs to the reception area where everything was in darkness. It did not bother me to find my way in the dark, since I already had a good image of the layout of the building in my mind. I found the switchboard on the desk in reception and was horrified when I saw how many buttons and switches covered the main console panel. There was no way I was going to be able to switch it through to my room and did the only thing possible. Feeling rather guilty, I picked up the switchboard's main receiver and dialled Carol's number. I was worried that a member of staff may find me using the telephone system and tried to be as quiet as possible.

To my relief, Carol answered. I quickly explained that I could not stay on for long since I was phoning from reception. She seemed happy to have heard from me and that I was safe. After just a few minutes, I wished her a goodnight and promised to phone the following day. I went back to bed, happy in the knowledge that I had accomplished my mission without attracting the attention of the staff.

The next day was to bring new experiences I had never before imagined. There were just six students being taught at any one time and, as it happened, I was the only male in the group.

Amanda Spearing, the tutor, was an attractive young woman who had the unenviable job of transforming six people who were all terrified of the water, into proficient swimmers. When I saw how she glided through the water, I was impressed by her grace and skill. I felt determined to do everything she asked of me and, hopefully, not disappoint her.

The benefit of this course was that nobody was embarrassed by our inability to swim since we were all at the same stage. The size of the pool was just right and, for most of the area, it varied only between four and five feet deep. There was a step down to eight feet at the deep end, but we all kept well away from that part of the pool. All of us wore goggles, including Amanda, to protect our eyes from the chlorine. Those who wished to could also wear a nose clip, which I found preferable. I could never understand how anybody not wearing a nose clip could swim without getting water up their nose.

The first task was to get us all in the water. Once there, we were asked to hold our breath and try to sit on the bottom of the pool. It was surprising to find how difficult it was to sink to the bottom. The only way we could achieve this was to jump up first and use the weight of our bodies to help us sink. Even so, it was impossible to stop oneself from quickly bobbing to the surface again. This was made even more fun when Amanda threw rubber rings into the pool for us to retrieve from the bottom. How I wished I could have had the courage to do this when I was a child. Ever since I was, as a boy, pushed into a swimming pool by a supposed friend, I had lived in fear of drowning.

As we gained more confidence, Amanda showed us how to float, tread water and the basic strokes. The fact that I could not see her very clearly did not matter. She was in the water with the rest of us for most of the time and patiently described what I was doing wrong. As we swam along, one at a time, she would even swim backwards and below us. As well as seeing exactly what we were doing, it was a great confidence booster.

On the twenty-fourth of November, during my course, I was saddened to hear the news about one of my favourite singers, Freddie Mercury of Queen, one of the best groups ever. His death was, apparently, caused by bronchial pneumonia, as a consequence of Aids. The television news was, understandably, dominated by Freddie's demise and all of us on the course were in shock.

By the middle of the week, when she felt that we had improved, Amanda changed the rules. Up until that time we had been swimming across the width of the pool, each person having an imaginary lane of their own. The change was that we had to swim, in turn, from the shallow towards the deep end. Amanda assured us that she would stop us, long before we reached the deeper water. She was standing at the turning point, urging each swimmer to keep going. Since I was the only male, I normally went first for anything new, but, unusually, she had all the others starting before me.

When it came to my turn, I began swimming breast stroke towards her. “Keep those arms going, John. Don’t forget to use your legs. Keep going! Keep going!” she instructed, her clear voice echoing around the pool. As I kept striving to reach her, I thought it seemed to be a long way. To my astonishment, I reached and touched the far end of the pool. As I grabbed hold of the rail, Amanda and the other women all clapped and cheered. I felt so elated at my achievement that I was speechless as well as breathless. “I knew you could do it, John.” For once in my life, someone had actually shown confidence in my abilities. I could have kissed her for what she had helped me to achieve, but I thought I had better resist the temptation. Apart from anything else, I now had to launch myself from the deep end and head back towards the shallows. I was surprised how more buoyant I seemed to be in the deeper water and, after taking a deep breath, I managed the return journey without difficulty.

The lessons were forty minutes long with an eighty minute break and there were just three lessons each day. Although we could use the pool at other times, most did not have the energy to spend all day swimming. During each afternoon, Amanda did provide massage for any of the pupils who chose to pay the fee, which I thought to be reasonable. I took advantage of the service and had a half hour massage for most afternoons. She was really good and I certainly felt very relaxed and at ease after each session. She would make conversation during the massage and, very soon, we knew quite a bit about each other. When I told her of Carol’s changeable emotions, she felt that I was probably wasting my time with her and should find a more worthy companion.

Every morning and night, I telephoned Carol and had a long conversation without revealing the purpose of the course. She was curious, but I was determined to make her wait. As usual for Carol, her mood changed a great deal from day to day. She had felt low at times, but had managed to resist the temptation to open the sealed envelope.

As the week progressed, I really felt that I was achieving some degree of competence and still tried everything Amanda showed us. I found underwater swimming much easier than I had imagined, and amazed myself by swimming, under her instruction, between Amanda's legs, without knocking her over. I found the whole experience great fun and made the most of my time.

The biggest test of my courage was on Thursday, the last day of training. Amanda asked if anyone would volunteer to jump in the deep end. Initially, the thought horrified me. Eight feet of water was two and a half feet deeper than my height and a cold chill came over me at the thought of it. Still, Amanda would not let me drown, I reasoned. Apart from anything else, it would give the school a bad reputation. One of the women students and I volunteered for the ordeal.

First of all, Amanda showed us just what to do. She stood right at the edge of the pool, held her arms outstretched and just stepped in. She did disappear under the water, but soon reappeared and swam to the side. She reassured us by saying that she would stay in the water. In true gentlemanly manner, I let the woman pupil go first. She stood and tried to pluck up enough courage, but found she could not do it. I knew it had been mean of me to make her go first and offered myself as the guinea pig. I knew the longer I waited, the worse I would feel, so I did not hang around for long. As I stepped into space after taking a deep breath, the water seemed to rush up at me, enveloping my whole body. I sank swiftly to the bottom, but very quickly rose to the surface once again, my outstretched arms stabilising me. From there, I swam to shallower water. I felt so pleased at yet another achievement in this eventful week. My success spurred the other student to follow suit and she equally found the experience exhilarating.

On the following day, the final crunch was to come when Amanda tested each student on the skills that had been taught over the past few days. To ease our minds, she did say that she would take our efforts during the week into account, just in case we were nervous of the test itself. Amanda put us all through swimming breast stroke, back stroke, underwater swimming, treading water and floating. One thing she did not test us on which I had come to enjoy was somersaulting in the water. Still, I felt reasonably happy with my efforts.

We were all asked to assemble in the dining room to receive our certificates. All twelve students from the two groups were waiting, somewhat nervously, for the presentation to start.

Amanda would say a few words about each person in turn and then present them with their certificate. As everyone applauded, the student would give Amanda a kiss of gratitude on the cheek. She went through this for the other group first and then called each of my group next. I realised that she was calling all the women first, which, although quite correct, meant that I would be last. Since I was, by nature, a shy person, I was apprehensive about being last. I was not prepared though, for what Amanda said, as it came to my turn. "And now, finally, for someone who I feel has to be the star pupil. I can honestly say, that I have never enjoyed teaching anybody as much as I have with John. For someone who arrived here afraid of water, he has achieved so much in one week that he has good reason to be very proud of himself." I am certain I must have blushed at such an accolade, which I definitely had not expected. I walked up to her, with the sound of everybody clapping, thanked her warmly and gave her a kiss of gratitude.

That same afternoon, I had booked an hour's aromatherapy with Amanda and, as I lay on the couch, I said, "What you said about me this afternoon was very sweet, Amanda. I do appreciate it." She smiled warmly and continued to massage the sweet-smelling sandalwood oil into my body. Over the past few days, during my massage sessions, she had asked me if I had a woman friend and I had told her about Carol and our somewhat stormy relationship. She, like my secretary, Birgit, thought that I should finish with Carol to prevent further anguish. I knew they were right, but

I could not imagine life without Carol, no matter what she had done to me. As I relaxed, thanks to Amanda's soothing hands, I felt very happy and contented.

The meal on that evening was to be a special celebration event.

The whole staff pulled out all the stops and made and served a superb meal, two of the girls even dancing a can-can at one stage. Afterwards, all the students gathered in the lounge for an evening's celebration.

Although everybody knew each other by now, I did feel that the evening would still be a very quiet, restrained event. I felt I should do something to liven up the evening and had a quiet word with the young woman who served the drinks. I asked her to provide two bottles of champagne for the students, but to say that it was a gift from the management.

I knew that two bottles between twelve would not go far, but, in conjunction with the wine which everyone had been drinking, it did have the desired effect. Everybody relaxed and chatted happily, several of the women becoming quite merry as the evening progressed. Many jokes were told and the room echoed to the raucous laughter of the intoxicated group.

At one point, discussion turned to the size of the bedrooms at the school. Eventually, it was suggested that we go on a tour of the rooms comparing their lack of space. After looking at the tiny, cramped rooms in which some of the women were staying, I came to realise that my own room was spacious by comparison. They agreed and told me that I seemed to have had the best deal of all. We all had a laugh at a toilet on the top floor which had to be entered through a door which was only about five feet tall. The room itself was extremely narrow, but about twelve feet in length. The toilet was the solitary piece of furniture at the far end of this corridor like room.

Another talking point was the cost of using the school's telephones, the amounts only coming to light when the bills had been issued during that afternoon. "I only made a few calls and it's cost me eight pounds", said one of the women.

"Yes, it's ridiculous", another agreed. "They've charged me twelve pounds." Everybody knew that I had been phoning Carol regularly and one of the women turned to me and said, "How much did yours cost, John?"

I was hoping they would not ask. "A hundred and fifteen", I replied. There was a stunned silence and people froze with glasses half way to their lips.

"You're joking. It can't have been that much for just five days, can it?" one of them asked incredulously.

"I'm afraid it is. I have spoken to my girl friend every morning and night, sometimes for nearly an hour." I was aware that the school would make a surcharge as a hotel would, but, where Carol was concerned, cost had never been an obstacle.

I heard one say, "I don't know what they could have to say that would take that long." I suppose it must have been obvious that I was very much in love and no further questions were asked about the cost of telephone bills.

Breakfast, the next morning, was the last time we met as a group. I had a final, solitary swim in the pool early that morning and felt pleased with my progress. I was, by no means, a strong swimmer and I knew that I still had a lot to learn, but, at least, I could now swim without fear.

I was pleased when Amanda called at the school, that morning. It gave me a chance to thank her, once again, for everything she had done for me. We talked in the bar for a few minutes and then I gave her a final, parting kiss. She had a lovely, cheerful nature and I hoped that, someday, I would see her again.

The taxi arrived to take two of the other students and myself to the station. We said our farewells to other students and staff and started our journey home. I prayed that British Rail would not let me down, since I had arranged to meet Carol that afternoon. Fortunately, it was an uneventful journey and I reached my home around four o'clock.

Carol arrived, just as I was about to dress after a refreshing shower. I pulled on my housecoat as I rushed down the stairs to let her in. It seemed ages since I had seen her. We kissed and hugged as we went upstairs to my bedroom. There, I continued dressing as we talked.

"Are you going to tell me what this course was, now?" she asked with obvious curiosity.

I slid my fingers into my half-packed case and retrieved my swimming certificate. "Just read that", I said proudly as I handed it to her.

Her eyes swiftly scanned the contents of the official-looking document and she exclaimed, "John, you're wonderful. I never would have guessed that you were on a swimming course. That's marvellous, darling."

"I hoped you would be pleased. I won't be long, now. I must just put some clean clothes in my case." She watched, patiently as I finished dressing and re-packed my case. It had been a bit of a rush, but I was soon ready. "Right, I'm ready now. The taxi should be here any minute."

It was on time and took us the few miles into the centre of Manchester and dropped us off at the imposing entrance to the historic Midland hotel. Most of the patrons at this hotel would have alighted from BMW's, Mercedes or Rolls, but our mode of transport did not make me feel at all inferior. I always felt like a million dollars when I was with Carol anyway, but I had never been afraid of mixing with wealthy people. I knew they were no better than me and proudly walked through the revolving doors into the huge reception hall. I had been in many hotels, but the atmosphere and unashamed luxury of this hotel made it my favourite.

We booked in as man and wife, but, of course, Carol had to fill in the registration details. The staff must have wondered why I did not do it myself since they could not tell that anything was wrong with my eyes. As long as I had an escort, then my handicap was not obvious to anyone. We were escorted to our room by a porter who carried our two overnight cases.

Carol went into raptures over the room. "Darling, it's lovely."

She opened all the doors to see what was behind them. "Hey, there's a mini-bar." As she studied it, she realised that as soon as anything was removed from the fridge, the cost was automatically added on to our bill. More importantly, there was a huge bed and a lovely bathroom.

Unusually, our first priority on that night was to put on our swimwear and head for the pool. We took the lift down to the lower ground floor and followed the signs to the leisure club. This was the first time I had visited this centre at the hotel. Exercise bikes lined the wide corridor which led towards the changing rooms and the desk where we collected our towels. It was not long before we were in the pool together.

The one disappointment was that the pool was so small. At its deep end, the width was reduced by a Jacuzzi, making it one of the smallest pools I had seen. Still, it served the purpose of showing off my new-found skills. As Carol swam in front of me, I swam underwater and tried to follow her legs. I suppose I showed off a little, demonstrating how I could adopt a mushroom shape underwater and floating on the surface in the star formation.

Carol was impressed and kept saying, "John, I think you're wonderful."

I replied, "If it hadn't been for you, I wouldn't be able to do this now. I needed a good incentive to make me lose my fear of water. I would do anything for you, love."

She smiled, gave me a hug and said, "Yes, I know you would." She looked around the pool and said, "The Jacuzzi's empty. Let's go in there for a while."

As we sat in the hot, foaming water, Carol took hold of my hand and placed it on her breast. Someone else did come in the Jacuzzi but, with the opacity of the turbulence, they could not see my hand caressing Carol's breasts. She was so sensitive there and always liked to feel my hands gently teasing her nipples. Her own hand moved down between my thighs, caressing the steadily-increasing bulge in my swimming trunks. I felt certain that, to any observer, it would be obvious that both Carol and I were sexually aroused, a fact which heightened our passions even further.

We decided that enough time had been spent in there and, after drying and dressing, returned to our room. Our clothes did not stay on for long. We stripped naked and held each other close. I ran my fingers lightly over her buttocks as I kissed her with a fiery passion. She shivered with excitement and pulled me on top of her. Unlike the first time we made love when I was not prepared, I now kept a good stock of condoms and always had some close at hand. Carol reached under the pillow, tore the foil and swiftly slid the condom on my erect penis. She was so practised at doing this, that it was almost an automatic reaction. As she parted her legs to allow me to enter her vagina, she said, "Hmm, that's lovely. Oh, you're huge, tonight."

"That's what you do to me. Making love to you is out of this world."

"Do it really hard to me, tonight, darling. Really hard." I did not need much encouragement and took long, hard, thrusting strokes. Strong enough to make the bed creak noisily. "Oh, that's lovely. Oh, yes, yes!" she almost shouted the words as we climaxed. We lay there for a while, partly for me to get my breath back after my exertions. My heart pounded furiously for several minutes and beads of perspiration ran down my back.

We washed and, once again, dressed. I had booked a table in the restaurant and both of us, by now, were feeling quite hungry. We linked arms and walked along the corridor and down in the lift to the ground floor. This hotel had three restaurants, but, that night, we were going, for the first time together, to the French Restaurant.

This had a reputation as being one of the best in Manchester and tables had to be booked a week in advance. As we entered the candle-lit room, the head waiter asked my name and escorted us to our table. The room was very high, with a ceiling at least twenty five feet above floor level. With the low level of illumination, even Carol had difficulty in reading the menu. When a waiter offers me a menu, I will always accept it and pretend to be reading it, although, in reality, Carol would be reading to me. Of course, this menu was in French, but, thankfully, there was a description of each item in English. Once we had decided what we were having, the wine waiter assisted us in choosing a suitable choice of drink.

The company, the food and the service were all superb. As soon as our glasses were nearly empty, a waiter would appear from out of nowhere, take the bottle out of the ice-bucket and fill our glasses. It made me realise just how much we were being observed as we had a very intimate meal. As we had always done before, we shared each other's meals. There were other people in the restaurant, but the tables were spaced well apart, helping to make conversations very private. Relaxing background music was provided by a pianist playing a grand piano just outside the entrance to the restaurant.

We took our time over the meal and, after fully satisfying our appetites, we thought that a walk through Manchester city centre would be a pleasant end to the day before going to bed. It was a fine, yet cold, November evening as we crossed the road towards Central Library and into St. Peter's Square. All the Christmas decorations and lights gave a welcoming atmosphere to a city which is not normally renowned for its attractiveness. Carol loved me to walk her through the city centre, mainly, I suppose, because it was such a sharp contrast to her own small North Wales town of Mold.

Our journey took us down towards Deansgate, along past Kendal's towards St. Ann's Square and then back along Cross Street. With our cheeks flushed from the cold, night air, we returned to the warm comfort of the hotel. The huge hall was still bustling with scattered groups of overdressed and, in some cases, somewhat pompous people. We quickly passed through their midst and headed for our bedroom. The very thought of spending a whole night with Carol and not just a stolen hour or two, excited me beyond belief. I realised that, one of the things which made Carol so special, was the way she made every touch, every kiss, every act of love seem to be so illicit. It was as though she was my mistress and, yet, she was free to do whatever she wanted and with whom. I think the fact that she had chosen to be with me rather than Dave, who had obviously played such a large part in her life, made me feel so very special.

We undressed and, once again, made beautiful, passionate love. The difference, this time, was that, after the exertions of our prolonged love-making, we could lie naked, holding each other close and just fall asleep. I did stay awake a little while, listening to Carol's steady breathing, a sound I loved to hear. It was mainly because it showed that she felt comfortable with me.

CHAPTER NINE - DECEMBER, 1991

I think I awoke first, the following morning. It was Sunday, the first day of December. I put my arm around her and gave Carol's warm, naked body a gentle squeeze of affection. Drowsily, she stretched, gave me a squeeze and said, "Hmm, 'morning, darling."

"Hello, love. How did you sleep?"

"Oh, I had a lovely sleep. I feel so comfortable with you. Everything seems so right. Would you like a drink of tea?"

As I agreed, she slipped out of bed and turned on the kettle. She was standing there, completely naked, calmly making us a drink as though it were an everyday occurrence. I was pleased that she did not have any inhibitions about her body when we were together. She was quite a shy, modest person in front of other people, but, with me, she did not mind being naked at all.

We sat up in bed having our drinks while we reflected on the events of the previous evening. As though to gain the advantage of every waking moment, we quickly finished our drinks and then started petting again. This time, she was on top of me, moving her body in a rolling motion with my penis pressed hard against her pubic area. She even placed it between her breasts at one stage, continuing to move her agile body to stimulate both of us with maximum effect.

Afterwards, we both stepped into the bath, turned on the shower and washed each other's bodies. A perfect act of mutual intimacy; something else for me to treasure for the rest of my life.

Unfortunately, this precious moment in time had to end shortly. We dressed, went down to reception and settled our account, after Carol had inspected it for any inaccuracies. A taxi was called for us and we returned the few miles to my house. There, we had a drink of coffee and, although we had not had any breakfast, Carol could not stay any longer. She had to return home to collect the children from her former spouse. I often wondered how he must feel, knowing that, no matter what story she may have told him, she was obviously spending the night with another man while he took care of the children.

Once again, I was left on my own as her car sped away from my house. The depression always returned as soon as we parted, mainly because I never knew when I would see her again, if at all. That was the worst uncertainty I had to suffer. Would there be a call from her in a couple of days time saying that she could not see me again, just as she had done six months earlier? That had been after our first beautiful weekend together. I knew that, with Carol, nothing was guaranteed.

That night, for the first time, Carol was in my dreams. I did not know how significant it was, but I did find that she occupied my thoughts for much of the time. We talked on the telephone morning and night again, but, by Tuesday, there was, yet again, a change in her mood. She accused me of pressurising her, simply because I asked when I could see her. She had turned my suggestion of taking her away on holiday to Florida in February, to one of my being selfish and only satisfying my own needs. She had clearly forgotten the circumstances in which I had offered her something special to look forward to.

She must have had second thoughts about taking the boys with us and said that, although we would go away, it would be on our own. I really did not mind whether we took the children or not. Without them, we would not be as restricted for love-making whenever we wanted, but I would have sacrificed that to go away as a family. Since I had not yet met the children, I was a bit nervous about meeting them, but, if it made Carol happy, I would do anything for her. What I did not realise then, was the extent to which she preferred me not to meet them.

Towards the end of that week, when I phoned her late at night, her phone was engaged. This was very unusual and I had a strong feeling of apprehension. When I did get through to her about twenty minutes later, she said that one of the boys had knocked the phone off its hook without anybody realising. I was not convinced by her explanation, since there would be a howling noise after only a few minutes of disconnection. I was hurt that she felt she had to lie to me. After all we meant to each other, I thought I deserved more. I knew I would not achieve anything by expressing my disbelief and just ignored the temptation. I felt very unhappy as she, once more, suggested that I see another woman to take the pressure off her. As if to reinforce her attempt to distance herself from me, she told me that she did not love me, and that, if she had given me that impression at any time, she had only been 'acting'.

It was so obvious that she had met someone else. Within the space of one short week of spending a beautiful weekend together, she had, once again, rejected me and made me feel worthless. There was nothing I could do at all except carry on with my life as normally as possible. The trouble was that, whenever she had rejected me in this way, I always slept badly and my health seemed to suffer. How could one woman have such control over me? It seemed that, with Carol, I was destined to fluctuate between idyllic happiness and severe depression.

I stayed with my parents for the following weekend. They were thrilled at my success in swimming and asked me about all the events during the course. My father had always been good at swimming and was particularly pleased with my new-found success. Over the past two years, I had noticed that my parents had begun to show a pride in me, which boosted my self confidence. Feeling unable to go for a day without speaking to Carol, I asked my parents if I could phone her. They did not mind at all, but I did not stay on for long in an effort to keep the cost to a minimum.

Carol had said that she would come to my house on the Sunday of the following weekend, but yet again made excuses at the last minute for not coming. How I wished that my eyes were good enough to drive, then seeing her would be so much simpler. It would take two trains and a taxi for me to travel to her place and, on a Sunday, that would not have been very easy. I had to spend yet another miserable day missing her. Since I knew that I would not be able to see Carol over Christmas, as she would be staying with her sister and her family, I knew I must see her this week to give her a Christmas present. Even for this, she seemed reluctant, but agreed to see me on Wednesday afternoon. I took the train to Chester and met her at the station entrance. She had some Christmas shopping to do and asked if it would be alright if we did it together. I did not mind at all, as long as I was with her. We only had about an hour before the shops closed, but, in that short time, we passed through many places without buying much at all. After this, we relaxed for afternoon tea in the dignified atmosphere of the Grosvenor Hotel. During our conversation, she admitted that Dave had begun telephoning her again. Even though she had told him not to contact her, she knew that she still loved him. I really wished that she would accept that he was no good for her and forget him. We exchanged Christmas presents, had a quick drink at the Queen's Hotel and then returned to the station. Just three hours together was all that we had on that day and I knew that I would not be able to see her for some time.

Friday was to be a new turning point in my life. I was determined that I would not be spending Christmas at home on my own and, since Carol would be with her relatives, I just had to go away for a holiday. Early in November, I had booked to travel to Singapore and now the time had come for me to start my holiday.

My secretary drove me in the SAAB the few miles to Manchester Airport and helped me find the information desk.

Once there, I assured her that it would be alright to leave me and wished her a happy Christmas. I gave my name and flight number to the person at the desk. At the time of booking, I had made it known that I was visually impaired and was seeking assistance during my travelling. I had always found all airport and flight staff superb at helping to make travel a pleasant experience and, on this occasion, I was not disappointed. I was escorted to the correct check-in desk, where my luggage and documentation were handed over.

The worst aspect of airports is the length of time one has to sit around, just waiting. At least, I had no worries at all since my escort took me through customs and, when the time was right, came for me to guide me right up to the entrance of the plane. There, very attractive, Singaporean stewardesses took over. One found a seat for me and made certain that I was comfortable a few minutes before the rest of the passengers boarded the plane. It was a huge Boeing 757, but only about a hundred passengers embarked at Manchester. This did mean that, once the flight started, several stewardesses had some spare time. The plane was flying first to Paris, where the rest of the passengers would embark. During that short time, I was given fantastic assistance and company by three attractive stewardesses. I would certainly travel with Singapore Airlines again, if this was a sample of their hospitality.

I was even more surprised and pleased when two of them, quite independently, offered to meet me in Singapore on Christmas Day. I told them which hotel I would be staying at and one of them gave me her address and telephone number. They seemed impressed that my visual handicap had not been an obstacle to travel, especially on my own. There were two empty seats at my side, but this proved to be useful, particularly when a meal was served. These two friendly stewardesses, whenever they had a spare minute, would stop and chat as well as tell me what was on my tray and where everything was to be found. I was impressed by the gracefulness and beauty of all the female cabin staff.

They wore full-length, richly patterned dresses which seemed to emphasise how slim and petite they all were. If they had to bend at all, such as when serving meals, they would bend at the knees, rather than the waist. All of them seemed to be very attractive with long black hair, narrow hips and small, nicely shaped breasts.

It seemed a shame when we touched down at Paris and the three stewardesses I had come to know so well in that short time had to leave the aircraft as it was the end of their shift. Once they had collected their own luggage and put on their long, thick, winter coats, they returned to wish me a pleasant journey and a good holiday. The plane did fill up at Paris and the new cabin crew, although very helpful, did not have the time to socialise. The whole flight from Manchester to Singapore lasted fifteen hours, but it was not an uncomfortable journey. I did manage to sleep, but not very soundly and was pleased to see a beautiful dawn breaking during the long flight.

Even the meals were far superior to any I had previously experienced while flying.

On arrival at Singapore, I had to wait until all the other passengers had disembarked, but I did not mind. As the cabin crew said goodbye to me, a young woman from the airport was waiting to act as my escort. Once she had taken me through customs and baggage collection, she looked for the travel rep. It did not take long. A very pleasant Indian Singaporean called Norani, met me and led me out of the airport to a waiting minibus. It was a beautiful, hot sunny day with temperatures in the eighties; a noticeable contrast to what I had left behind in chilly Britain.

The bus stopped at several, huge hotels, dropping off its passengers. Norani told me that my hotel would be the last stopping place. There was only a couple of other people in the bus with me as it pulled up outside the magnificent Oriental Hotel. Porters took our cases as we walked over the wide, red carpet and through the main entrance door. The door was held open by a tall, coloured man who was dressed in long bright red coat, top hat and white gloves. I imagined that, considering the temperature, he must have been very hot and uncomfortable. I must admit, that the idea of holding doors open for people all day, must be one of the most boring of occupations but, still, he looked happy enough.

What I saw next took my breath away and I was grateful that I still had enough sight to appreciate it. I did know that the hotel was twenty-one storeys high, but the scale of this building was visible from the inside as well as out. There was an absolutely cavernous atrium, extending to nearly the full height of the building. In the middle of this wide, open area there was a hollow column running from top to bottom. Around the outside of this column, four glass capsules slid smoothly up and down, ferrying people to the various floors. At each level, a walkway connected the lift column to the gallery running round the inner perimeter of the building. All the bedrooms and function rooms ran around the outside of the building and were accessible from the galleries. To add to the magical effect, each successive floor was smaller than the one below it, giving a tiered outline to the galleries. I did not appreciate it at the time, but the design of the building was based on that of a shell turned upside down. The final extravagant touch was the extensive use of multi-drop chandeliers and cascading water. The scale and imagination, I thought, made the architecture of modern British hotels look like biscuit boxes, by comparison.

Reception was on the third floor and my room was on the eighth. It was a twin bedded room with every conceivable luxury one could wish for and a huge picture window looking towards Singapore harbour. Air conditioning made the room comfortable, belying the sweltering temperatures outside. I wished that Carol could have been with me to share this experience of a lifetime, although, if she had, I would have insisted on a double bed.

I did not feel as though I was suffering too much from jet-lag, but I was tired and slept for an hour after I had unpacked. It was now early Saturday evening and after having a light meal in my room, I called reception and asked if someone could show me around the hotel. The place was so enormous that I did not know how I was going to find my way around. To my surprise, the assistant-manager came to my room and brought a young Chinese Singaporean woman called Ivy with him. He apologised for not having time to show me around himself, but said that Ivy was available to help me. I was impressed and graciously accepted his offer. Ivy spoke in a precise, cultured English, something which was sadly lacking in most English people, particularly in the Manchester area. I asked Ivy if she would show me the controls in the lifts, since I was going to have to use them many times. Each of the glass-sided lift capsules had its own magnificent chandelier and a control panel with an absolute array of buttons. There would be four levels I needed most, for ground floor, reception, leisure centre and my own room. To cover all of these, I memorised their relative positions starting from the bottom of the panel.

Once that had been taken care of, we went to the ground floor, where Ivy introduced me to the concierge. Next, she showed me how to get to reception, where I met the other staff. There were several restaurants in the hotel, so we went to each and Ivy would tell me typical prices and comparative menus. I was determined to use my new-found swimming skills on this holiday and asked her to show me where the pool was. Unusually, it was not in the basement, but on the fourth floor. Since it was about ten o'clock at night, the pool, approached through the leisure centre reception, was closed, but, at least, I now knew where to find it. I was building up an overall map in my mind of the places I needed all relative to my room and, finally, we returned there. She was very much at ease and sat on my bed, talking for a while, answering my questions about Singapore and asking some questions about Britain in return. After she had left, I went to bed and slept soundly on my first night in this strange country.

I had found out that the pool was open at seven and was there prompt and on time. The night before, when I looked through the glass doors of the leisure centre, I had not appreciated that I was not looking into a room and had quite a shock when I walked through the doors and into an area which led to the open air. A very attractive, young Chinese Malaysian woman, wearing blue shorts, white tee shirt and trainers approached me. She was, apparently, in charge of the Poolside Restaurant and a lifeguard for the pool itself. A beautiful smile lit her face as she asked if she could help. I explained that I intended having a swim first and then would have some breakfast. I also told her how I was still a novice at swimming and asked her how deep the pool was. It was a huge pool and, unusually, its depth increased across its width to a maximum of eight feet. I decided to stay towards the shallower side and stepped into the water. It was a lot cooler than I had been used to, but it was quite an experience to be swimming in an outdoor, unheated pool during late December.

About forty minutes of practising my strokes were enough and I decided my stomach needed some sustenance. I pulled a long, towelling robe on and sat at one of the poolside tables. Again, this very pleasant young woman came over to me very promptly. "Did you enjoy your swim?"

"Very much, thanks. I'm going to try and have a swim first thing every morning before the pool gets busy." She gave me a menu. Politely, I explained that I did not see very well and was unable to read it. From that moment on, she could not do enough for me. Her name was Angeline Kew and, during my ten day stay, she was a perfect angel. She helped me with all my breakfast meals and provided she had enough time would come and talk to me while I was eating. Sometimes, she would even crouch by the side of the pool while I was swimming. I was very flattered when she asked if she could write to me when I returned home to England.

The idea of having a pen friend in Singapore appealed to me and I readily agreed. An indication of how keenly she was watching me came when I asked her about the preserves on the breakfast table. Of the three pots in front of me, there was only one which I liked. She told me they were always in the same order, mine being in the middle. A couple of days later, I was about to open the middle jar when she rushed up to me. She was full of apologies because, on that day, they were in a different order. I was truly impressed by her attentiveness and happy in the knowledge that I had managed to make yet another friend. A friend who, hopefully, would stay in touch for many years.

At nine thirty, I went down to the ground floor and met Norani Bte Ali, the travel rep. A coach tour of Singapore had been organised, which took most of the morning. In addition to showing the major features of Singapore, we stopped for a while at a crocodile farm. This was quite fascinating, with different pools for different sized creatures. I was thankful that the area was quite secure, keeping observers safe from the hungry-looking crocodiles. Afterwards, I returned to the pool, had lunch and sunbathed for the afternoon.

Even with the beautiful, relaxing surroundings and very warm, friendly people, I still felt a longing and need for Carol. She would not have yet left to travel to her sister's, and I decided to phone her. Singapore time was eight hours ahead of Britain, so I waited until ten at night, hoping that she would be in for an early Sunday afternoon. To my relief, she answered the phone and was surprised, but pleased, to hear my voice. For the next ten minutes, the thousands of miles between us disappeared to nothing as we chatted happily.

When I awoke the following morning, dull, threatening clouds hung heavily in the oriental sky. December is one of the rainiest months in this part of the world, so it was not surprising. I rushed down to the pool and managed to get about twenty minutes swimming before the heavens opened. The huge canopy extended mechanically to protect the people eating in the poolside restaurant, from the downpour. An excursion to the island of sentosa was planned for this morning and I felt certain that I was going to be soaked. With temperatures still in the eighties, I decided to wear as little as possible and had on shorts, sports shirt and trainers. This seemed to be the ideal solution, since there was not much to dry when the downpour eased.

Cable cars took me, along with my party, over the sea and

onto the island. Sight-seeing around Sentosa was made easy by travelling on a mono-rail. It was a beautiful, tropical island, but, unfortunately, I was not seeing it at its best, thanks to the rain. I decided that, if possible, I would return to this island again during my holiday.

Back at the hotel, I was getting a little more adventurous with my eating and had my evening meal in the Chinese restaurant. A helpful waitress told me what was in all the many little dishes spread out in front of me. Although I was not used to such spicy dishes, I did enjoy my meal.

During my visit to the hotel's leisure centre, I had discovered that a massage service was available and decided to see how it compared to what I had found in Britain. I had booked it for a quarter to nine that Sunday evening. To my surprise, the massage was to be carried out in my room, something that would not be considered in Britain. My meal had taken a little longer than expected and I realised that I would be a few minutes late. As soon as I could, I rushed back to my room. It was a pleasant surprise to see a tiny, Chinese-Singaporean girl standing outside the door to my room. I quickly let her in, apologising for the delay. She was wearing only a brief, white, one-piece tunic, similar in style to a swimming costume. I wondered if she was available to provide more than just a massage, but decided that I must resist any temptation for intercourse.

As far as I was concerned, Carol was the only person I wanted to make love with. In addition, I remembered my promise not to have sexual intercourse with any other woman. Her name was Jasmine and, I imagined, she was probably no more than eighteen years old.

I began to undress as she unpacked her bag of oils and lotions. "How much do you want me to take off?" I asked, a little nervously.

"Everything, please", she answered, with a wide smile. I gulped at her reply and realised that this was going to be very different to anything I had experience before. When Amanda at the swimming school massaged me, I did keep my briefs on.

Obediently, I stripped completely and followed her instruction to lie face down on the bed. She did place a towel over my buttocks to ease my embarrassment and asked me to open my legs. While I was lying in this somewhat vulnerable position, she climbed onto the bed and knelt between my legs. From there, she was able to apply maximum pressure to massage my lower back. For her small size, she had a lot of strength in her arms and hands. After completing that part of my anatomy, she asked me to close my legs a little, while she moved to kneel at my side. From there, she was in a good position to massage my legs, running her nimble oiled hands high up my inner thighs, creating, not surprisingly, an extremely high degree of sexual arousal. In addition, on several occasions, the back of her hands would, tantalisingly, touch my testicles lightly. Although I still had a brief covering of a towel, I found it embarrassing when she asked me to turn to lie on my back allowing her to work round the other sides of my thighs. I tried to think of anything non-sexual to reduce the size of my erection. I tried, by remembering my bank account codes, passwords and telephone numbers, but it was all to no avail. She certainly must have seen my strong erection , but, thankfully, never commented. I did talk to her a little, but she seemed to be concentrating on her work. At least, that's what I thought she was concentrating on. For nearly an hour, she worked on almost every part of my body. when Jasmine was massaging my shoulders, she was, again, kneeling on the bed with my head between her thighs and close to her crotch. This had to be the most exciting and erotic massage I ever had or was likely to have.

Even my skull received some attention. When she was finished, she re-packed her bag, asked me to sign a receipt and wished me goodnight. I certainly felt very much better for her attention and slept very soundly that night. On most occasions when I passed through the leisure centre on my way to the pool during the rest of my holiday, Jasmine would be at the reception desk and always gave me a big smile. The thought that she was one of the few women who had seen me sexually aroused inevitably gave me an extra tingle of excitement, mixed with a degree of embarrassment. For her young years, Jasmine must have seen many equally excited, naked men. I decided that I must have another highly erotic massage from Jasmine, before the end of my holiday.

The next day was Christmas Eve and, for this day, Norani had offered to show me some of the shops and help me, wherever possible. First, we went to a department store, where I was measured for a suit and then returned to the hotel. I did know that there was a shopping area below the ground level of the hotel, but I had not appreciated the extent of it. It was a complete shopping mall extending much further than the area of the hotel and probably a great deal of Orchard Road. As well as shops, there were several cafes and even a children's fairground called 'Magic World'. Norani was married with two small children and, quite naturally, brought them to this place as a treat. We went on one of the fairground rides together and laughed at our juvenile activities. Much to her amusement, I 'arm-wrestled' with a mechanical Samurai warrior, and lost.

By this time, it was late afternoon and we were feeling a little hungry. I offered to buy her a meal, which she gratefully accepted. After a pleasant meal, Norani offered to write some postcards for me. I told her that Carol was my girl friend and asked if she would mind writing a card to her as well as my parents and Amanda from the swimming school. She was happy to do all these for me. We stayed in the restaurant while I dictated and she acted as my temporary secretary, a role she seemed to enjoy. I felt very lucky that I had all these women friends who seemed to be prepared to spare some time for me.

Later that evening, I had booked to go on a Chinese Junk for a Christmas Eve celebrations and a meal. This was disappointing since there were not enough people on board to create any festive atmosphere.

I had a pleasant surprise when I returned to my hotel, later that night. A couple who I had met on my first day, Brenda and John, invited me for a drink in the Captain's bar in the hotel. Although it was very busy and noisy, I enjoyed their company and stayed talking until one thirty. On the stroke of midnight, everybody cheered to welcome in Christmas Day and an attractive young woman gave each person a kiss.

I did not wake up in time for an early morning swim, thanks to my late-night drinking, but I did not mind. I had a lazy morning and when it was mid-afternoon I telephoned my relatives in Britain to wish them all a merry Christmas. This was the day that I was supposed to have my date with the stewardesses. I had been wondering what I would do if they both wanted to see me at the same time, but, since I had not heard from either, I wondered if I was going to be disappointed. I decided to telephone Wendy, rather than wait to be called. A very sleepy voice answered. She was, apparently, suffering from jet-lag, but assured me that she would be fine and refreshed by evening. Wendy told me that, if she had not been so sleepy, she and her flat-mate were going to cook a meal for me, at their home. Instead, she asked if they could both come to the hotel and dine in one of its restaurants. This sounded great to me and I readily accepted.

When I received a call at seven o'clock to say they were in reception, I eagerly left my room to meet them. I was stunned by their amazing beauty when I saw the two, young women approaching me. Both wore close-fitting, black, glittering cat-suits. The only difference was that Wendy's suit was sleeveless. Both had beautiful, long, black hair which rested seductively on their shoulders, were very slim and petite. Wendy was twenty six and her flat-mate, Meeling, was only twenty three. I walked in the middle holding their hands as we made our way to the Chinese Restaurant. This was truly like heaven and I realised that this holiday was the best I was ever likely to experience. In the well-lit restaurant, I let them suggest what type of food I should try and we all chatted openly. I did not feel uncomfortable at all with them and tried to give the same attention to both women.

When the meal was served, I was provided with a knife and

fork, but traditional chopsticks were also available. I did try, but was absolutely useless at eating in such a way. To show off their skills with chopsticks, the two women fed me a few mouthfuls of food. I could not keep a straight face for thinking of what this scene must have looked like to the other people in the restaurant. Any possibility of these two beautiful, young women just using me for a free meal was dispelled when Meeling insisted on paying for the meal. This was to celebrate her recent promotion to chief stewardess at the age of only twenty three instead of the usual twenty five.

We had a drink in the Captain's bar after our meal and, this was where I met Felix, a friend of theirs. He drove us, in his car, to another hotel which had a club called the Crescendo.

The two women quite often visited this place, as it held Karaoke evenings. This was my first visit to such a place and I was surprised how good the visitors to the club sounded, when they chose to sing. People who were singing stayed at their tables and had a microphone handed to them. If someone wished to sing, they wrote their name, table number and chosen song on a slip of paper and handed it to the organiser.

After a while, the microphone was brought to our table and handed to Wendy. She sounded superb as she sang the Carpenter's song, 'Yesterday once more'. It was even more touching, since she inserted my name into the song and looked affectionately at me throughout. This was a fantastic evening and I wished it could last much longer. It was two thirty in the morning when Felix drove us back to my hotel. Wendy came into the hotel foyer with me and left the other two in the car. She walked with me to the lift. It was with great sadness that I realised this would probably be the last time I could see her, since she would be flying to other countries the following day. I held Wendy's body close to my own as we kissed. It was a delightful, enticingly deep, soft, lingering kiss. Her small, firm breasts pressed tantalisingly against my chest and I felt a longing, deep inside of me for her. It was not to be, though. She had to return to her friends and wished me goodnight, saying that she would try to be at the airport on the day of my departure. I did wonder just what her feelings were towards me, but, for a first date, she appeared very warm and affectionate.

When I called at reception for my room key, I discovered that a message had been left for me. It was from the other stewardess who had said she would meet me. She apologised for not being able to come and wished me a happy Christmas. I was disappointed, but hoped that there may still be a chance of seeing her. As I lay in bed, the memories of this fantastic evening, seven and a half hours of absolute bliss, filled my mind as I kept re-living Wendy's passionate kiss. I imagined her naked and in my bed, exciting me with her lithe, supple body and small, sensitive breasts. Would she be as good as Carol?

Although I did not fall asleep until after three that morning, I did not have chance to sleep late. I still had a swim and breakfast before being ready for an excursion which purported to follow in the footsteps of Raffles. He was an Englishman who had a significant effect on Singapore in the nineteenth century. The tour ended at the Raffles Hotel, where I enjoyed a Singapore Sling, a delightful, refreshing drink. It was a cocktail, consisting of gin, cherry Heering and Dom Benedictine, diluted with fresh pineapple juice and was, initially, created by Ngaim ng Boon, a bartender at the Raffles Hotel in the early nineteen hundreds.

During late afternoon, Norani called at my hotel to act as escort on a private excursion. This was to be an adventure in eating, since our destination was Newton's Circus, an open-air food market. Unfortunately, there was a torrential downpour at the time. We did borrow an umbrella from the concierge at the hotel, but still managed to get quite wet. The passage-ways between the stalls were like rivers as the tropical storm continued throughout our meal. There was a timber roof above us, on which the rain pounded heavily, but the building was open-sided, letting in much of the rain. It did not spoil our enjoyment, though, as Norani had me sampling barbecue crab, sting-ray, chilly crepe and many other hot, spicy foods. I had said that I would try anything provided I could have a long, cool drink to help ease the burning to my soft, western palate. The chilly crepe, in particular, brought tears to my eyes. I still enjoyed the whole experience and felt very grateful to Norani for giving up so much of her time.

I had to miss my swim the following day, since I was booked on an excursion which left the hotel at seven thirty. It was a long, hot coach journey of five hours to Malacca in Malaysia. Once again, I was lucky enough to make friends with our travel guide, Aisha. She was a petite, beautiful, young woman who came from Malaysia and was probably in her late twenties. The road through Malaysia was narrow, fairly straight and seemed to go on for mile after mile.

Travelling at night was, apparently, quite hazardous, thanks to the lack of road lights, as could be seen by several abandoned vehicles in the ditches at the side of the road.

The journey was broken when the coach stopped at a typical country house. All the passengers were allowed to wander through this home which was actually occupied by a perfectly ordinary family. I was pleasantly surprised by the standards of the house and felt that, in many ways, it was superior to those found in Britain. Every passenger received some fresh, Mauritius pineapple, which I found to be the sweetest, most wonderful pineapple I had ever eaten.

When we reached Malacca, we walked through the narrow streets with Aisha telling us about the history, culture and religion of the city. She did warn the tourists not to photograph any elderly women, since their superstition made them believe that it would age them even more, hastening death.

For those of us who felt fit enough, we could make a long climb up a hill by many steps, from where we could all see for miles over the surrounding area. After a tour of a Dutch Christian Church and a meal in a good quality hotel, we started our long journey back. Since Aisha was not giving a commentary for the return journey, she invited me to sit next to her allowing us to pass the time by chatting to each other. I felt very fortunate that, somehow, all these beautiful, attractive young women actually sought my company. It did cross my mind, that God might be testing me to see if I could remain faithful to Carol.

Despite making so many new friends and enjoying my holiday, I was still missing Carol and she was in my thoughts a lot of the time. I would have given anything to have her with me, especially in my bed. It seemed ages since we had been able to make love and I knew that having sex with someone else would not make me feel any better.

The next day was spent much more leisurely, mainly sun-bathing by the pool. During the afternoon, Norani arrived at the hotel and, this time, brought her two small children with her. Her six year old daughter and four year old son seemed to accept me as a new friend very easily, especially when I gave them some candies which I had in my room.

I had asked Norani if she would assist me in buying a present for Carol and she had offered to go with me to a gem factory. Even before embarking on my holiday, I had decided to buy Carol a gold chain while I was in Singapore. Once we were at the factory, we toured the cases of beautiful, finely sculptured chains. There was such a wide selection, that I found it difficult to make a choice. Norani was about the same height and build as Carol and proved to be very helpful in acting as a model. As well as the chain, I bought a jade pendant to complete the gift.

They had cost more than I had intended paying, but I knew that Carol was worth every penny. She was one of those women who men wanted to spoil and shower with gifts.

Norani had brought a camera with her that day and used a complete film, taking pictures of her two children and me. We visited Magic World again and all enjoyed ourselves on the various rides and amusements. The two children were wide-eyed with the excitement of their outing and clung tightly onto me with their tiny hands. Norani introduced me to them as their new uncle, an honour I was quite pleased to accept.

My holiday was now nearing its conclusion and I had not, as yet, returned to the island of Sentosa. I was determined to go and tried to organise a personal guide, but without success at such short notice. Although Norani was not able to escort me herself, she found a solution to my dilemma on my last day. Her nineteen year old sister, Rosenita, and a school-friend were happy to show me around the island. We toured the precious stones museum, butterfly gardens and a museum which chronicled the history of Singapore, in particular the Japanese invasion and liberation.

Probably the most enjoyable place, though, was the Aquarium. This was very different in its concept, since the visitors were encouraged to relate more closely to the exhibits than usual. In particular, there was a slowly moving walkway on which the observers could stand while being surrounded by fish and sea creatures of all different types. It was quite an experience to see the white belly of a shark gliding smoothly just a few inches above your head. The two girls seemed to enjoy this as well and asked another visitor to take a photograph of us. I had my arms around their waists while the bright, aquatic world acted as a backdrop. I was surprised how thin Rosenita was, but she seemed to be a happy, carefree girl.

We had a meal on the island and it was while there that I realised just how I had lost track of time. It was seven thirty and, at nine, I had to be at the hotel reception, ready to check out and travel to the airport for my flight home. In that ninety minutes, we had to take a ferry back to the mainland, travel by taxi to the hotel, pack my suitcases and check out. The ferry seemed painfully slow, but I did not feel in the least concerned. Rosenita saw a long queue of people waiting at the ranks when we arrived at the mainland, but, somehow, she managed to commandeer a taxi. The two girls giggled excitedly as we raced back to the hotel. I had just fifteen minutes left as we pulled up in front of the huge building.

Realising how little time I had left, Rosenita asked if there was anything she could do to help. I said that it would be quicker if she and her friend could assist with the packing, which they both quite happily agreed to. In my room, the two girls helped to ensure that I had everything in the right place and to make certain that nothing was left behind. I quickly changed into more comfortable travelling clothes and arrived at reception with just two minutes to spare. I checked out and met Norani, who had to organise my travel to the airport. I thanked the girls for the fantastic day with them. I knew that I would miss all the new friends I had made over the past ten days and genuinely felt sorry to be leaving Singapore.

I did hope that the stewardesses would be at the airport as they had said they would, but I was to be disappointed. There was no sign of them as I boarded the plane after saying goodbye to Norani. During the sixteen hour flight, I did make friends with another stewardess and even managed to visit the flight deck under her guidance. It was a very dark area with the displays of numerous dials giving the area an eerie glow. This was yet another first experience in my life and one which I would always treasure. The plane did stop at Istanbul on the way back, where I was surprised to discover that it was snowing. Manchester Airport was not particularly welcoming either, but there was no snow. One short taxi journey and I was home once more.

It was nine thirty in the morning of New Year's Eve and, desperate to hear Carol's voice, I phoned her within minutes of arriving home. She seemed to be pleased to hear from me, much to my relief. I was becoming accustomed to the fact that she was so unpredictable and often worried about her reaction every time I called her. We talked for a little while and then I began to unpack my cases. I was tired after my long journey and did not do much during that day. It was quite amazing, therefore, how quickly my tiredness disappeared when the phone rang shortly after six in the evening and Carol's soft tones reached my ears.

"Would you like me to come and see you, tonight, John?" she asked, much to my amazement.

"Yes, that would be great. What time would you like to come?"

"About eight. I'd like to go into Manchester. Do you mind?"

"No. Of course not. We can probably find some New Year celebrations." This was fantastic news. I busied myself, tidying the house, had a shower and dressed ready for my date.

When she arrived, I greeted her with a big hug and a kiss and then gave her the present.

She eagerly opened the parcel and exclaimed "Oh, John, darling. It's beautiful. Can I wear it tonight?"

"Of course you can. There's nothing I'd like better."

"How do you like my new dress?" she asked, turning around to let me see it fully.

"Mmmm.., it's lovely." I lifted the hem and felt the material. It was a short, V-necked dress, mid brown in colour, but the material was so soft that I could not tell what it was made of. "What material is it?"

"It's silk." Carol did have a very good dress sense, if somewhat expensive. She did look good and the gold chain and jade pendant suited her well.

We drove into Manchester and went to our favourite hotel. As expected on a New Year's Eve, the restaurant was full. We just stayed for a quick drink and then went to look for somewhere else to eat. After quite a search, we managed to get a meal in an Italian restaurant near to Deansgate.

What she told me, that night, shocked me. First of all, Dave was now phoning her every day. Since she had told me only four months earlier, that she never wanted to see or hear from him again, I found it difficult to understand why she was letting him call. She had told him that she would not see him until he had left his wife, but I wondered if she would change her mind on that as well. He had sent her a Christmas card and present, but she had not sent anything to him.

She felt certain that he would never leave his wife.

There was still worse news to come. Since the middle of November, she had been dating another man. I felt sick at this revelation. I had always said that she must tell me the truth, no matter how painful it may be, but she had only decided to tell me now because he had finished with her. The reason he had given was that another woman he had known for some time had re-appeared on the scene. I wondered if that had been genuine or did he realise that Carol was not trustworthy? I recalled the time she had said the children had knocked the phone off the hook and felt certain that this new man was the real cause of the engaged tone. She had been out with him several times and, so, must have lied to me about her outings, probably using her woman friend as the scapegoat. The only consolation I had was that she was now no longer seeing him, but how long would it be before she found someone else?

I told her about my holiday in Singapore and the new friends I had made while there. I did not feel that I had cheated on her the way she had on me as I had not wanted to form a serious relationship with any of them. Carol would always be the first and the last woman in my mind. I wondered if she would have seen me that evening if her new relationship had not ended.

We walked to Albert Square to see large crowds of people gathered in front of the Town Hall.

It was a cold but fine night and the crowds seemed to be in good humour. As the clock struck midnight, fireworks exploded around the square and loud cheers echoed from building to building. I held Carol close and gave her a long deep kiss. "Happy New Year, love." I said this hoping that she would be more faithful to me in nineteen ninety two. After a final hug, we returned to the car and headed for my home. How I wished she could stay the night, but, as usual, she wanted to return to her own home.

CHAPTER TEN - JANUARY, 1992

We talked on the phone late on New Year's day for almost an hour and a half. During this conversation, she told me a lot more about the man she had been seeing. I did not ask how intimate they had been in case I did not like the answer, but it was a question which constantly caused me some anxiety. In truth, I did not mind how many friends she had as long as she reserved her love and intimacy just for me. This, coupled with the re-emergence of Dave, made me feel distinctly uneasy and uncertain about my future with Carol. If I had not been so much in love with her, I think I would have ended our relationship at that time. One little sign of encouragement came when Carol told me that she was thinking of changing her telephone number to prevent Dave from continuing to call her. Since I knew Carol so well, I realised that there was every possibility that she would not actually do anything about changing her number, but, at least, she was thinking about it.

I was disappointed when she told me that our planned holiday in February may not be for the whole week and perhaps just a few days. I could see what she was doing. She had an appointment during the week, which I felt certain was a deliberate attempt to reduce our time together. Given a little more time, she would probably find reasons why we could not go away at all. She knew that she was letting me down and said she felt guilty but, what I could not understand was why she did not realise that she was really letting herself down. After all, my suggestion for the holiday in the first place, was because she wanted to get away from the cold, British winter to a warmer climate and wanted something to look forward to. She was infuriating at times when she implied that, in seeing me, she was doing me a favour. She was far more blind than me, at times.

I was even more despondent when she told me that Dave had been to her house and with her permission. This was the woman who hated him so much, wanted vengeance for being abandoned by him and had vowed never to see him again. She had even asked my advice as to what she could do to him as an act of revenge, but I had managed to convince her that she should not seek to do such things. Why could she not see that he had already wasted far too much of her life? Even she could not ignore the fact that he was still married and did not seem to be making any effort to start divorce proceedings. I was certain that, in Carol, he saw her as being no more than a mistress and she was worthy of a much better status.

My only consolation was that Carol had said she would go with me to the theatre on the following Saturday. The only problem was that there were no seats available for the show we both wanted to see. Tom Courtney and Polly James were starring in 'The Miser' at the Royal Exchange Theatre in Manchester and it was proving to be a very popular play. Staff at the box office suggested that I keep phoning to see if there were any cancellations. From early Saturday morning, I phoned the theatre at ten minute intervals in the hope of catching a pair of tickets. I was beginning to think that it was an impossible task when, shortly after two o'clock, I was told that two tickets were available for the afternoon matinee. I eagerly booked these and phoned Carol straight away to tell her the good news. She had been prepared to settle for going to the cinema, if necessary, but was pleased at my success.

Carol had hoped to arrive at my house for three thirty, but was about half an hour late because of heavy traffic. When she did not arrive on time, I was worried for her safety. It was unlike her to be late, but I felt very relieved when, at last, she arrived.

"Are you not angry with me for being so late?" she asked as we drove in her car towards Manchester.

"Angry? Why should I be angry? You could not have known what the traffic would be like. No, I was worried about your safety, that's all." She explained that her ex-husband would have been furious with her, no matter whose fault it had been. She must have led a miserable life during her marriage if she was so nervous about upsetting him. No wonder she had not been able to resist the temptation to have an affair when Dave appeared on the scene.

We did miss the first ten minutes of the show, but managed to pick up the thread of the story. It was the first time we had been to the Exchange Theatre and it was an experience which should not be missed. Unlike traditional theatres, it was a 'theatre in the round' where the audience completely surrounded the stage. It struck me as a good test of an actor if they could convey the story without the benefit of elaborate stage sets. Carol and I were at gallery level, as usual holding hands, and thoroughly enjoying the whole spectacle. Tom Courtney played the part of the miser superbly and, at times, successfully brought the audience into the act.

I had booked a meal for after the show, and, as we drove towards the area of Piccadilly in Manchester, Carol was telling me how much she had enjoyed the play. Her favourite theatre was still the Palace, but all of them had a magic that television could never achieve. We left her car in the Piccadilly Hotel's roof-top car park and walked through the automatically opening doors and into the large reception area. The restaurant itself was cosy and intimate, though we agreed that it still was not as good as that in our usual hotel. Since it was a relatively modern building, it did not have the atmosphere or grandeur we had now become accustomed to.

We drove back to my house after an enjoyable meal. There, my hopes that Carol would stay for the night were dashed when she said that she would have to get back for the children. I wanted to make love, but she would not even stay for that. This was the woman who had asked me not to have sex with any other woman because she would satisfy all my desires herself. This was yet another promise Carol had broken. It was six weeks since we had made love and it was her own fault that I now had a sexual appetite greater than what she was prepared to satisfy.

After this date, we continued our telephonic romance, talking to each other late at night. It was shortly after this that we had our longest conversation yet at nearly two hours. We talked about anything and everything, but it was very rare for us to be short of something to say. Carol even said that she wished she could love me enough to marry me, because everything felt so right with me. Even though she had said this, I knew she would never actually marry me. As long as she was searching for the same feeling she had for Dave, nobody else would ever stand a chance. She managed to hurt me most when she repeatedly wished that she could meet someone else who would generate this same feeling.

I felt particularly uneasy when she told me that Dave's wife was going away for a week. I was certain that she could not resist the temptation to be with him. I have no doubt that, if she did, I would be told that she was seeing Barbara, her best friend. This, in her way, was to stop me from being hurt, but, in reality, she just could not stop herself from telling lies. Unlike the truth, lies are self-perpetuating.

I do not know how I would have managed to see Carol as much if Manchester did not have as many theatres. She did seem to be attracted to some of the productions around at that time and, when Arthur Miller's 'Two Way Mirror' was showing at the Library Theatre, she agreed to come. It was the last Saturday in January and a really cold day when she arrived at my house again. Since it would be late before we had our meal, she brought some sandwiches to satisfy our appetites.

It was after we had finished our snack that we started kissing and petting. When suggesting what time she should come to my house, I had deliberately allowed enough spare time to avoid having to rush to the theatre. Although I realise that sex is possible in just a few minutes, that was never my style. I liked plenty of foreplay, slow, tender love-making and time afterwards to just hold each other close. She always loved to precede intercourse with me kissing deeply, teasing her nipples and sucking her breasts. Her excitement would be aroused to such an extent by this that she would be climbing over me, hot and desperate for me to enter her. On most occasions, we would both spend part of the time on top. It seemed to bring the wildness out in her when she was on top of me and her supple body would be writhing in a frenzy of passion.

It had been two months since we last made love and, like me, this long interval only seemed to fuel her desire for arousal. Her sighs of ecstasy grew ever louder as we neared our climax. It was at this point that she liked me to be ever more forceful, thrusting my penis harder and harder inside her. The sweat would pour off me from my exertions and, after our climax, we would both collapse exhausted on the bed. I was envious that she always seemed to get her breath back quicker than me, but, felt certain that, if we were able to make love more frequently, I would stay in better condition. For me, it was certainly the most energetic exercise I was currently accustomed to.

Once Carol and I had recovered, we dressed again and drove into Manchester. We parked near to Central Library and, as we were doing so, Carol noticed a lot of police in the area as well as large crowds of people. To our surprise, the crowds were gathered in front of the Midland Hotel, our favourite hotel, where we would be eating later in the evening. Jokingly, we decided that they must have been waiting to greet us.

Carol was curious about the reason for the crowds and asked a police officer just why they were there. He told us that there was to be a ball at the hotel, that evening, in honour of the Holcombe Hunt and the crowds were animal rights protesters. I had never known Carol to be so curious about anything before as she watched the protesters who had been prevented from getting too close to the hotel's entrance by makeshift barriers. After one last look, we entered the Library Theatre and took our seats, ready for the performance. It was, in effect, two short plays, and very unusual ones at that, but we still enjoyed them.

It was after ten, when we crossed the road to the hotel, in front of which, there were still crowds of protesters braving the cold, January evening. Not surprisingly, they did not present any obstacle to our entrance, as we walked into the massive hall and turned right towards the Wyvern Restaurant. We only dined in the expensive French Restaurant on very special occasions and, on this night, we chose to dine in the Wyvern. I often wished that Carol would run her toes up and down my legs as she had done the first time we had dined in a Chester restaurant together, but she did give my leg a squeeze every so often. If we were sitting opposite each other, I would, occasionally put my leg between hers and rub our calves together. We still fed each other at every opportunity.

During our meal, I told Carol that I had received a letter from Wendy Fok, one of the stewardesses I had met on my flight to Singapore. I was surprised when she expressed a feeling of jealousy over me having correspondence with a woman twenty years younger than her. Since I had told her everything about my Christmas Holiday and knew that I had not cheated on Carol in any way, I did not have a guilty conscience about anything I had done. I told her that she need not be jealous, since she was the only woman with whom I was in love.

The restaurant was practically empty when we left, shortly before midnight. Back home, I wanted to show her an Oriental picture which I had bought from Singapore for my parents. I was looking for this in my wardrobe and, as I was searching through the shelves, I felt Carol's arms around my chest. She pulled herself close to me and tightened her grip as I stood up. While I had been looking for the parcel, she had slipped her dress off and was wearing only bra and knickers. She unfastened the buttons on my shirt and unzipped my trousers. Stepping out of them, I turned to face her and removed her last garments. Her breath was quickening as we kissed and stroked each other's bodies. I felt that special little shiver of excitement as I ran my fingers lightly over her smooth, rounded buttocks. She had already found a condom under my pillow and skilfully slid it onto my erect penis.

"Do it hard again, darling. I love it when you are forceful." The bed creaked noisily as our bodies pounded the mattress in a delightful rhythm of erotic pleasure. This time it was not to be slow as she urged me to come quickly as she was ready. The climax soon came as our bodies tightened and twisted in waves of sexual relief. "Oh, that was wonderful. I love you so much, John." She held me tight as our hearts pounded against each other. We stayed like that for a few minutes until Carol decided she would have to go.

She pulled on her clothes and gathered her things together. I slipped on my housecoat and followed her down the stairs. How long would it take before she stayed for the night? I could not understand why she had to go, since the children must have been staying with her ex-husband. With a final kiss, she wished me goodnight and climbed into her car. I told her to drive carefully and walked back into my empty house.

It had been a perfect evening but, sadly, it was now over and I did not know how long it would be before we could enjoy each other again. It was nearly one in the morning when I checked the time. Thinking about the protesters in Manchester, I switched on the radio to see if they were mentioned on the local radio news. To my surprise, the newsreader did refer to scuffles as animal rights activists protested against the Holcombe Hunt. When Carol phoned me on reaching her home, I told her of the radio news. We were both very tired and wished each other sweet dreams as we settled down for what was left of the night.

When I spoke to Carol the next evening, I was pleased that she had taken my advice and told Dave not to call her again until he had done something definite about his divorce. I was still convinced that he had no intention of leaving his wife and, hopefully, would not be bothering her again. I had a feeling, though, that it was unrealistic of me to expect Carol to forget her longing for Dave. Even though I was certain that she loved me, I think Dave had, unwittingly, sabotaged any future relationships she may have.

Fortunately, I did manage to find the present for my parents, which I had been looking for when Carol so delightfully distracted me. I had invited my parents to come for a meal that day and gave them the oriental picture during their visit. They listened spellbound as I related my experiences while in Singapore.

That week, the closed circuit television, which I had been using for only a couple of months, broke down. There was a crackling noise and a strong, acrid smell pervaded the whole house. In that short time, I had become very dependent on the CCTV, since it helped me to read all sorts of diagrams, tables and handwritten notes necessary for my computer business. Both the CCTV and the Kurzweil personal reader had become an integral part of everyday life. Before I had the CCTV, I could only see such documents by using a strong magnifying glass, but, over a period of time, this was becoming ever more difficult and tiring. I had to manage without the CCTV for a few days, until it was replaced.

Since I had not yet met Carol's children after nine months of seeing her, I thought it was time to get to know them. I suggested that we all go to Manchester's Granada Studio Tour as it would be interesting for everybody and an easy way of meeting them. Although Carol seemed quite keen at first, she rejected the idea after giving it some thought. It seemed as though she was frightened of the consequences of us coming together. I just could not understand her reluctance and felt hurt that I seemed destined to remain her secret lover. She did not even want me to tell my relatives anything about her; not even her name.

CHAPTER ELEVEN
- FEBRUARY, 1992

I was thankful that Carol was, at least, still letting me see her and waited eagerly for Saturday, the first day of February. On that day, I travelled by train to Chester, where Carol met me at the station. We found a little cafe in Chester, where we stopped for a coffee and Danish pastries. On many occasions when we were on a date, Carol would phone her children to make certain that they were alright and she did this several times on that day. This was to be the first time that we were to go to the cinema together. The film, JFK, was showing at the Cannon Cinema in Carol's home town of Mold in North Wales. I did find the cinema more difficult to follow than the theatre, but I would never let this become an obstacle to my enjoyment.

With my narrow, limited field of vision, I had to 'scan' the screen to make up the picture in my mind and, if it was a fast moving, action thriller, this would be impossible. Provided that the narrative to a film was good and there were not too many silent parts, I could usually follow it.

In this case, I did miss some messages the film was trying to convey, but Carol would explain these, if I asked her.

The three hour film was very thought provoking and controversial, but we both enjoyed it. In fact, for the ten months I had known Carol, we had not had a bad date. She would always complement me on my organisational skills. I would never chance on getting into a show or a restaurant and, to avoid disappointment, would always book as far ahead as possible.

We had booked a meal in a large hotel not far away and found the meal there provided the perfect end to a superb day together. Well, almost perfect. I would have much preferred to book a room for the night, allowing us to sleep together. I longed for the time again when we could just fall asleep after making love instead of one of us having to leave. It was shortly after eleven when the taxi arrived to take me home. This was the worst part of our dates when we had to separate. As soon as we were apart, I had an awful feeling as though part of me was missing.

We both realised that our dates were expensive and agreed that, to save costs, we would eat at my home on some occasions and stay there to watch a video. There was only one night of that following week that we did not have our usual telephone conversation. On the Tuesday evening, Carol was going to Birmingham with her friend, Barbara and her husband to see Eric Clapton in concert. I wished that Carol was not so secretive about me and then I could have gone with her to make up a foursome. She so wanted to be normal and not to be the odd one out, but her guilt, or whatever it was, would always be a barrier to this normality.

I was still hoping to arrange a holiday for Carol's half-term leave, but, as I had expected, she was finding more reasons why we could not be together. Her ex-husband was going away and could not, therefore, look after the children. What was once going to be a week in Florida, had now been reduced to just Thursday night. She knew she was letting me down, but did not seem to realise that she was also letting herself down. She was the one who had longed to get away, back in November. My role was merely to provide a means to an end.

One evening, when I phoned Carol at the usual time, her phone was engaged. This always made me very apprehensive, as I wondered if she had started a new relationship or was letting Dave talk to her again. When I did, eventually, get through, she was upset. Apparently, she had been arguing with her ex-husband. He did seem to be a very un-cooperative person. By talking calmly and rationalising the situation for her, I managed to ease her mind a little and helped her to relax. She really did seem to look on me as her therapist, at times, but, I did not mind.

I was hoping, though not expecting, that I would get something from Carol in the post on Friday of that week. To send me something on Valentine's Day would have been a nice little gesture of her feelings and appreciation of me. Not surprisingly, nothing arrived. I had arranged for ten, long-stemmed, red roses to be delivered to Carol's house early evening on Valentine's Day. I deliberately did not have my name put with the flowers and wondered if she would realise who they were from. If she was seeing anybody else, at that time, it would have presented her with a dilemma. Who should she thank?

To my relief, she phoned, shortly after six, to say how lovely the roses were. I asked her if she realised the significance of there being ten roses. I had to remind her that we had been seeing each other for just ten months. I always thought that it was the woman who remembered significant dates, but, apparently not, as far as Carol was concerned. Still, I was certain that her appreciation of my gesture was genuine.

I did not know it then, but St. Valentine's Day was yet to hold greater disappointment for me. During our late evening telephone conversation, I again raised the question of our so-called week's holiday which seemed to be shrinking further and further every time we discussed it. There was now only a matter of days before half-term started, making organisation of anything significant impossible. She would not consider the question of taking the boys with us. I asked if they could not stay with friends, instead. She made it quite clear that she had no intention of doing such a thing.

"There's no point, anyway", she said bluntly. "What's the point in going away together, when I don't love you?"

I was stunned by her coldness. "It's a fortnight since I've seen you and I miss you so much."

"You know, John, you make me feel like I'm providing Social Services when I see you."

There was not much either of us could say after such a cold, thoughtless comment. This was, without doubt, Carol at her worst. It was impossible for me to sleep that night as her words kept echoing through my head. In reality, I was the one who provided anything like Social Services. She had clearly forgotten the reason behind my suggestion of going away. Carol was the one who longed to escape and I was merely providing her with the means to achieve her desires.

Over the last four months, I had been her comforter, psycho-analyst and pseudo-husband on the many occasions when she had phoned me in an upset state. She had cried torrents of tears over the phone and I had never once complained. I had always listened patiently, soothed her and done anything possible to help. She knew that she could telephone me at anytime she wanted and I would always be ready to help. When I thought about it, all I got in return was the opportunity to make love with her on the rare occasions when she was feeling in need of satisfaction herself. Carol was a woman of short term pleasure and long term pain and I really did not know whether it was worth going on.

I again contemplated suicide, but told myself that she was not worth it. There was always a slight hint of optimism that, one day, I would find someone who really loved me. Someone who would respect my needs and be willing to give as much as she received. I knew that I was not a selfish man. Over the past three years in particular, I had matured a lot and was determined not to make the mistakes which had contributed to the breakdown of my marriage. Like not taking a woman for granted, making certain that there was plenty of communication and, above all, listening with sensitivity to what the woman has to say.

After what was a terrible night, I rose on the Saturday morning and typed a letter to Carol. In it, I thanked her for a wonderful, ten month romance, but, in the light of her comments the night before, felt that it had now come to an end. It was a difficult letter to write and tears filled my eyes as those words of finality were committed to paper. I wondered what I should do if she phoned and decided to leave the answer phone on.

The phone did not ring at all on the Saturday and I did not call Carol. During Sunday, Carol did phone twice and left a message, simply saying that she had called. Initially, I thought it best to leave the answer phone on and wait until she received my letter on Monday. As the long, lonely hours of Sunday passed by, I felt that, perhaps I had over-reacted and wished that I had not left the machine on. At least she had phoned me which must have meant something. When she rang again, I answered. She apologised for what she had said and I admitted to over-reacting. I told her of my letter which should arrive the next day, but said that, if she wanted to continue phoning and seeing me, then it was alright by me.

Over the next few days, which actually was the half term holiday, we continued to talk on the phone every night. I wished that we had been able to go away together, especially to somewhere warm. A week of sun, sea and sex with Carol would have been the perfect medicine for me, at that time. The only prospect I did have, was the possibility, nothing more, of seeing Carol on the following Saturday. Even this possibility seemed to diminish as the week progressed. The reason, though, was forgivable. At times, Carol suffered from a painful neck and this made driving for any distance uncomfortable.

Seeing an obvious solution to her problem, I said, "If you would like, I could meet you at Chester station and come to your place." I half expected her to refuse such a suggestion and waited for her reply.

"I don't know, yet. I'll see a bit nearer the time." At least there was a faint glimmer of hope with this reply.

It was not until late on Saturday morning that she phoned me and, to my great surprise, agreed to meet me at Chester. She had even bought a video cassette recorder and hired a video for us to watch. This, to me, was a major landmark. To be accepted into her home, though it had taken ten months to achieve, was something I had longed for.

I travelled by train to Chester late in the afternoon and walked to the station entrance. It was not long before Carol appeared. In less than half an hour, we drove the few miles to her home in Mold. What gave me most concern was how her children would react to me. I really wanted this first meeting to be successful and was determined to make every effort to make friends with them. It was not as difficult as I had imagined. Both boys were well mannered and friendly, making our meeting seem perfectly natural. Carol had obviously briefed both boys about my poor eyesight, as they helped me whenever necessary.

Another first was to eat a meal prepared by Carol. She was a good cook and everybody enjoyed the meal. Afterwards, we all watched the video in the comfort of Carol's living room. The film itself was not very good, but that did not matter. Just being together, almost as a complete family unit made me feel very happy. Carol had asked me not to be obviously affectionate. I respected her wish and resisted the temptation to grab hold of her and kiss her passionately.

I was particularly looking forward to the time when her boys would go to bed. A time, I hoped, when we could be more intimate, although, I realised, Carol might be uneasy about it. Making love would probably be out of the question, but I would happily settle for kissing and petting, that night. Even this was not possible, as Carol's mood changed as soon as the boys had left the room. She became very irritable and almost seemed to regret having invited me. Since I knew that I had not done anything to upset her, I was very puzzled at her strange reaction. Once again, she accused me of putting her under too much pressure. It was only when my taxi arrived, shortly after midnight, that she gave me a half-hearted hug and a lukewarm kiss as a parting gesture.

As I travelled home in the taxi, I felt angry at Carol for treating me in such a way and angry at myself for putting up with her ever changing moods. The journey was made worse by having a driver who did not know the way and a taxi which smelled strongly of cigarettes. When I had booked the taxi, I had explained that I had poor vision and could not help with navigation. I eventually arrived home at about one thirty in the morning, feeling tired, angry and depressed.

To give her some credit, Carol did phone me early Sunday morning to apologise for her behaviour the night before. Her reason, though, seemed to make her irritability even more inexcusable. Her other man, Dave, had, for the past few weeks, been phoning every day, much to my disappointment. Every day, that is, except Saturday, the day I was at her house. She had been worried that something might have happened to him. After all the vengeance and hatred she had spoken of when referring to him, I thought her concern was a bit misplaced. Especially when it had ruined our evening together. What made the whole situation worse, was THE FACT that she later discovered that he had phoned after all, but it was while she was meeting me at the station.

For the next few days, we played a 'cat and mouse' game. I deliberately did not phone her, although it proved to be a great temptation to resist. There were two anxious evenings when she did not phone, but she soon started ringing regularly again. Apparently, she was not sleeping very well and was waking sometimes at four in the morning. Could this possibly have been her conscience troubling her?

The one thing which thrilled me, that week, was to receive a letter. Not just any letter, but one with an air mail label on the envelope. It was from Wendy Fok, my air stewardess friend from Singapore. She wrote quite often from all over the world and I always looked forward to receiving her letters. It was the fact that she was thinking about me that made her letters so special. It would take me ages to read such correspondence, assisted by using the high magnification of my closed-circuit television camera.

Just three days later, yet another air mail letter dropped through my letter box. It was from Angeline Kew, the young woman from the leisure club restaurant, whom I met at the Oriental hotel in Singapore. That holiday had been one of the best investments of my life, since it had resulted in new friendships. Friendships which, in time, I hoped would be more rewarding and reliable than Carol's unpredictable love.

It was on the day I received this letter that Carol revealed something of her true emotional conflict during our telephone conversation. I had felt, for some time, that my poor vision was a major barrier to her giving her full love to me. She had previously denied this, but, on that night, said, "It would be different if we were already married before you had problems with your eyesight. It's different then - you can accept it."

"So, you wouldn't consider marrying anyone who had a handicap like mine? No matter how strong your feelings might be?" I asked, incredulously.

"I just know that I could not cope with looking after you as your sight gets worse."

"And yet, I would marry you, even if you had a leg missing. True love isn't affected by such things. Apart from anything else, I'm the one who will have to adapt. I've no intention of being a burden on anybody."

"I know you don't, John, and I do admire how you manage, but I know that I could never marry you."

At least she had spelled it out, but I felt that she was being so unjust in using my handicap as an excuse. This again, would have been a suitable point to end our relationship, but I could not bring myself to do it.

Less than a week after her hurtful comments, Carol gave me the impression that she needed me more than ever. It was shortly after five o'clock on a Friday morning, when the phone at the side of my bed rang, waking me with a start. The sobbing I heard from the receiver could be nobody else's. "What's wrong, Carol, darling?" I said, tenderly.

"I..I'm sorry to wake you, John. I feel so low. I wanted to

phone sooner, but did not want to wake you. I could not wait any longer."

"You mustn't worry what time it is. You know you can phone me at any time and I'll always be here to help you. Now tell me just what's worrying you."

She explained that she had let Dave come to her house the previous weekend and this had unsettled her more than ever. She still has a strong yearning for him, but he still won't give up his wife. She has now told him not to phone or call her again until he is really free to marry her.

We both agreed that he must not love her properly if he was not prepared to make this final move. He seemed to want her just as a mistress, while keeping his wife. One effect of all this emotional stress on Carol was that she had developed eczema on her face. It was a vicious circle, in that, the more she worried about it, the worse her eczema became. We talked for nearly an hour, until she seemed more calm and composed.

It seemed ironic that I felt as strongly about Carol as she did for Dave. It was as though our love was on parallel lines, never destined to meet. I was still wide awake when, an hour after talking to Carol, the phone rang again. The tears, the anxieties, the uncertainties had all returned. She did not want to go to the school because she was feeling so low. With a lot of patience and careful reasoning, I managed to convince her that she would feel far worse if she stayed at home. At least, by going to work, she would not have time to worry about her situation. She phoned me twice more later that same day, during the evening. I was pleased that she had taken my advice and gone into work. On that one day, we must have talked for over three hours and most of that time was spent in trying to console her.

CHAPTER TWELVE - MARCH, 1992

Over the next few days, it was Carol who phoned me and at all times of day and night. While I did not like her to feel low or depressed, she seemed so much closer to me when she felt this way. From my point of view, the worst aspect was that I did not know how long she would feel like this. Every new day brought with it the possibility that she would make some cutting remark or just finish with me. She surprised me, one night, by talking about the possibility of us living together. Even this, though, was said in the way of a compromise solution rather than a desire. She also talked of writing to Dave and telling him that their relationship was finally over and that he must not contact her again.

As the days went by, her depression lifted a little and, once more, she became less dependent on phoning me at all hours. This was partly caused by the distraction of having to act as host to a French student who was staying for ten days. She was having to think of things to entertain him and places to go. One place she was considering was to go to a football match with her children and their guest. The problem she had was the telephone booking, since she would be asked for a credit card number for payment. Carol had disposed of her credit card when she had realised how much money she had been spending. She knew that she did not have the self-discipline to keep the card and made do with cheques or cash. Seeing her plight, I told her my own card number so that she could use it when booking. This was a measure of my love and trust in Carol, this strange enigma of a woman. A couple of days later, she phoned and announced that she had spent a hundred and fifty thousand pounds on my credit card. I laughed and replied that I did not mind as it would give me fifteen thousand air miles. In fact, she had not used my card at all, since they had decided not to go to the football match, after all.

When the French student had left, her depression returned which meant that she, once again, needed a lot of moral support. She had actually written a letter to Dave in an attempt to sever the ties with him for good. It had not had the desired effect, though, as he had telephoned her two or three times since then. We both felt that the simplest solution would be to change her telephone number, but I had doubted that she would ever do this.

Again, she talked enthusiastically about us living together at the weekends. This would suit us both fine as we had plenty of work to occupy us during the week. We could alternate whose house we would stay in and, if they wanted, the children could stay at my house as well, since I had enough space. I expected that they would prefer to stay with their father, but I really did not mind where they chose to stay. I let Carol know that they would be very welcome if they wanted to come. She was pleased that I accepted them so readily as part of 'the package'.

I looked forward with great enthusiasm to the following weekend, as Carol was coming to see me on the Saturday. This, so soon after being told that she felt like a provider of Social Services when seeing me, was an indication of her variability.

She arrived shortly before two o'clock, collected me and drove us into Manchester. Her kitchen at home had recently been extended and she now had room for extra kitchen utensils. We toured several shops, taking quite a time to find the items she wanted. She kept asking if I was happy to wander around the shops with her. As long as I was with her, I did not mind where we went or what we did. She gave me the impression that she was not used to her men being so accommodating and continually apologised for taking her time. I even enjoyed going into dress shops with her as it gave me an indication of her tastes and fashions, most of which, I liked. What did surprise me was the cost of her clothes. I knew that she had expensive tastes, but two hundred pounds for a dress was far in excess of what I had been used to with my ex-wife.

The reward for my patience was to come when we returned to my house after this expedition. We had only been in the house a few minutes when we started kissing and petting. Making love with Carol was such a wonderful experience that it completely cancelled out any ill feelings I might have had for her. It never ceased to amaze me how sensitive her breasts were. She would writhe about in sexual excitement as I teased and sucked her erect nipples. She was always desperate to let me penetrate her shortly after starting this delightful love-play. By now, I had become used to the fact that, in preference to gentle love-making, Carol much preferred hard, very physically demanding intercourse. The fact that she responded so well and very vocal always had the effect of heightening my own arousal and, ultimately, satisfaction.

When we had rested, we dressed and returned, once more, into Manchester City centre. I had booked seats at the Palace Theatre, where Albert Finney was starring in the play, 'Reflections of Glory'. As usual, we enjoyed the play immensely and held hands for most of the performance.

This constant 'touching' was so important to me and Carol told me that it made her feel good as well. If I caressed the palm of her hand, she would arch it in obvious pleasure. It was much more than just a physical link as we both felt emotionally closer as we touched.

By the time the show had finished, we both felt hungry as we made our way along Oxford Street towards our favourite hotel in St. Peter's Square. Although it was after ten o'clock, having a meal in the Wyvern Restaurant at the Midland Hotel seemed to be the perfect ending to a beautiful day together. For a change, we opted to cook our own main course using hot stones at the table. It was quite an experience as we turned the slender pieces of chicken, pork and beef on the sizzling stone, trying to prevent the meat from sticking. It was almost midnight when we left the restaurant to return to my home.

I wanted Carol to stay the night, but, once again, she insisted on returning home alone. I never could understand just why she had to travel home so late, when she could have stayed with me. On many occasions, she had said how much she liked sleeping with me and, yet, she still managed to resist the temptation. I still lived in hope that this situation would soon change, but did not know how long I would have to wait.

On the following day, I reminded Carol to contact British Telecom to arrange for a new telephone number. She agreed that it would be the only way to stop Dave from contacting her, but I still had my doubts that she would actually go through with it. My suspicions were confirmed when she told me on Monday, only two days after I had seen her, that Dave had telephoned her several times and she had even phoned him at his office. Worse still, she had been expecting him to call at her house that evening. This made me feel sick that, once again, he was interfering in our relationship. She assured me that I did not have any cause for concern, but I still felt uneasy about the situation. When she phoned me the following morning, she said that he had not been to her house, but had phoned her. To my dismay, she had decided not to change her number after all.

My suspicions were aroused even more when, on the Wednesday evening, there was no reply as I rang her number. I tried until after midnight, but without success. I felt certain that she must be with him and slept very badly that night. Carol phoned me early, the following morning and apologised for not calling me. The reason, she said, was that she was very tired and had unplugged the phone so that she could sleep undisturbed. I found her explanation unlikely, but knew that it would be counter-productive to challenge her excuses. As long as she continued to see me, then I was not going to disturb the status quo.

The eczema on her face was quite bad, at that time, an

indication that she was under pressure. I could understand how she would be emotionally stressed, considering the situation she was facing. Trying to balance her affections between a man who only wanted her as a mistress and me, who would be prepared to give her everything, must have been difficult for her. If only she could have had the same feelings for me as she had for Dave, there would have been no problem. Given time, I felt this could be possible, but, as long as Dave kept re-appearing, it seemed unlikely that it would ever happen.

As the time was approaching when we intended spending the weekends together, Carol started to have second thoughts, much to my dismay. "What will the children think when they realise that we're sleeping together?" she asked.

"Hopefully, they'll realise that we think enough about each other for it to be alright." Her question had annoyed me and I could not stop myself from saying, "Don't forget that you had the children with you when you stayed at Dave's flat, for a week last August, and he's still a married man."

She could not argue against this statement of fact, although I did regret having been so blunt. "I suppose you are right, but they really don't know much about you."

I realised from this that, although we had been seeing each other for almost a year, Carol obviously had not told them properly about our relationship. "Listen, Carol, you must try and escape from this 'mistress syndrome'. We've absolutely nothing to feel guilty about. We are both adults, single and in love with each other. I'm sure the children will soon adapt to the situation and accept me as part of the family. Children are far more flexible and understanding than you give them credit for, you know." I knew she still was not happy about the situation, but desperately hoped that my reasoning would convince her.

A few days later, on the Saturday, Carol, once again, came to my house. She was particularly keen to come as I had managed to find something she had been looking for. Carol wanted a small, marble topped 'Bistro' style table for her kitchen, but had not been able to find one local to her area. With just a few phone calls, I discovered that a furniture warehouse in Manchester had exactly what she wanted. She was really pleased to be able to buy the table she needed and enthused about it for the rest of the day.

For a change, we were having an inexpensive evening together. Carol bought some easy to cook meals from the local supermarket and, for the first time, she prepared a meal in my kitchen. A bottle of wine helped to make this a most enjoyable meal. We settled down afterwards to watch the video of 'Thelma and Louise', both of us feeling very relaxed. This, to my mind, was the next best thing to being married, especially as Carol had agreed to stay the night.

We weren't particularly adventurous in our love-making, that night, but it was still as wonderful as ever. To be able to just relax afterwards without worrying about parting meant so much to me that I felt so happy. Carol fell asleep first and I enjoyed watching her body gently moving as she breathed deep, comforting breaths. The main achievement, I felt, was that she was actually sleeping in my very own bed, our bodies pressed close together.

The following morning, it seemed so strange, yet delightful, to wake up and find a warm, naked body cuddled up close to me. We showered, dressed and had a light breakfast. Carol had to collect her children from her ex-husband's and left my house at nine thirty. It was about half an hour after she had left, when I realised that she had forgotten some school books in my house. I quickly phoned Kate, my ex-secretary, to see if she had time to drive me to Carol's, during the afternoon. When Carol phoned to let me know she had arrived home, I told her of what she had left behind. She was annoyed at herself for being so absent-minded, but it eased her mind when I said I could take them to her house.

I think Kate quite enjoyed driving my SAAB for the journey to Carol's. It was a cold but bright, March day and the directions provided by Carol were easy to follow. The two women had not previously met and I wondered how they would react. Kate had seen what devastating effect Carol's rejection, in June the previous year, had on me and, not unreasonably, did not have any reason to like her. I had no need to worry, though, as she was polite and friendly as they met.

Since it was a bright, sunny day, Carol suggested going for a drive, in my car, through the Welsh countryside. I thought it was a great idea and was relieved when Kate offered to stay at the house while we went out. This was yet another opportunity in this wonderful weekend to be on my own with Carol. She drove me to a little village, where we parked the car and had a walk. It was a lovely, picturesque village with steeply sloping streets. As we were driving back to her house, after our walk, I wished we could stop in some remote spot and make love in the car. I had never yet made love in a car and the very thought of it excited me. I was to be disappointed, though. We did stop in a car park where we kissed and caressed, but it was obvious that Carol was anxious about being seen with me by someone who knew her. I could not blame her and knew that I was being unfair in expecting her to take the risk of being recognised in a compromising situation.

Back at Carol's house, she gave us sandwiches and coffee before Kate and I left for the journey back towards Manchester.

CHAPTER THIRTEEN - APRIL, 1992

Over the next few days, my relationship with Carol suffered a setback, and all this so soon after a fantastic weekend. Basically, she was still worrying about what the children may think about us sleeping together. I could not understand why she felt so ashamed of me and felt so depressed when she declared, yet again, that she did not love me. Especially when she had given the opposite impression just a few days earlier. She accused me of putting too much pressure on her to do things which she felt uncomfortable with. It was the first day of April when she said all this, but it was certainly no joke. My fears and depressions returned once more and I did not know what to do with myself.

Towards the end of that week, Carol announced that she was going to stay at her sister's for the weekend. It was to be an opportunity to escape and decide just what she wanted to do. I only had her word for it that she actually was going away and realised that it may just be a way of stopping me from contacting her. This was a bit ironic, really, as she had been telephoning me a great deal in recent times, an indication, surely, that she felt she needed me. I did get a call from her on the Saturday and felt curious about her location. I hated myself for not trusting her, but, when just one lie is exposed, doubts about everything she said would be inevitable.

I felt the need to escape from home, myself, and asked Kate, my ex-secretary, if she would like to go for a drive in the countryside. She readily agreed and we set off, during Sunday afternoon, with no firm destination in mind. We ended up at Knutsford and had an enjoyable walk through Tatton Park. Kate realised how low I was and perceptive enough to know the reason. She was always good fun and did her best to lighten my mood. Kate's Irish humour always meant that we had plenty of laughs and I found her to be someone who I could confide in. Although we were only out for about three hours, I was so thankful for her company and temporary relief from my misery.

My fears about Carol's likely decision were realised when she phoned on the Sunday evening after she had returned home. Carol had decided that her love for Dave was greater than that for me and felt that, yet again, it was time to end our relationship. Her longing for him was pointless as, it seemed quite obvious to me, that he had no intention of divorcing his wife to give him the freedom to marry Carol. She had even said this herself, on many occasions, but her feelings for him blinded her to all possible logic.

I knew it was pointless to reason with her and said that I would not phone her again. My depression at this situation affected my sleep and my power of concentration, something essential for my type of work. My secretary could always tell when things were not going smoothly between us. She told me that, whenever I was tired, my eyes turned a deeper shade of blue, something I had never realised.

I was surprised when, only two days later, Carol phoned me at four thirty in the morning. It always amazed her how quickly I was able to talk coherently, even though she had disturbed my troubled sleep. She apologised for the cruel things she had said at the weekend and asked me to forgive her. During the conversation, which lasted nearly an hour and a half, she gave me reason for renewed confidence in our romance. Given the time to think again, she realised how hopeless her desire for Dave was. She even admitted that, when she had been with him, she had never felt truly comfortable in the way she felt with me.

I decided to let things take their natural course and did not arrange to phone her, but simply left it up to her to contact me when she needed. It was very late, that same day, when she rang again. The emotional stress she was under increased the severity of the eczema on her face and she felt so conspicuous by its effect. We talked for nearly three quarters of an hour, a great deal of that time being spent by me reassuring her of my continued love, no matter what happened.

I did not hear anything from her for the next few days and desperately hoped she would call me, no matter what the time may be. To my relief, she did phone, again early morning. She told me that she had written again to Dave, once more telling him to leave her alone. She had even been leaving the phone disconnected to prevent him calling. As the school half term was approaching, the pressure on her from that area was easing and she was beginning to feel a little better. During the holiday, she was taking the children to her sister's, but promised to phone when she could.

Since there was no way that I could rely on Carol's continued affection, I felt that I should see another woman. Thanks to the introduction agency, I was able to arrange a date for the following Sunday with Sarah, a thirty nine year old divorcee from Macclesfield. As usual, when I did anything, I organised it thoroughly. First of all, I checked on hotels within a reasonable distance of her home, which had both a decent restaurant and a leisure centre. I then checked if it had a room for the night and if Sarah would like to dine there. A hotel at Knutsford seemed to provide the perfect solution and it did have vacancies. Sarah knew the hotel, liked the restaurantand readily agreed to meet me there.

The next task was to book the meal, a room for the night and arrange transport there and back. When I phoned Kate, she happily agreed to drive me to and from the hotel in my own car. If nothing else, this little adventure would be a distraction from being disappointed by Carol. I knew that my heart was reserved for her, but was desperately short of female company.

Kate arrived at my house very early afternoon and we drove the short journey to the hotel. Once there, a puzzled receptionist wondered why I had booked a single room when both Kate and I had turned up. To add to the confusion, Kate had to fill in the registration details for me. She then helped me to find the room and just had to have a good look. It was a double room, as is quite often the case when booking only a single. Most hotels prefer to get the single rate rather than nothing at all. The receptionist seemed a little relieved when she saw Kate driving away from the hotel.

I asked if someone could escort me around the building to familiarise myself with it and, in particular, to show me the leisure centre. For the rest of the afternoon, I enjoyed myself swimming and trying out the apparatus in the gym. I did not usually try such things, but an attendant showed me how to operate the various items of equipment.

At seven fifteen, I was in the lounge bar, waiting for Sarah. The unusual feature of this bar, was its height. The people serving behind the bar were obviously standing at a lower level, which, from the customer's side, looked very strange. When Sarah entered, she recognised me from my description and walked over to my table, kissed me on the cheek and sat down. I ordered a drink for her and we began chatting happily. Unlike Carol, she had no ties since her only son was at University. She was petite and quite attractive with shoulder length auburn hair. She seemed quite relaxed and we talked happily without awkward pauses.

We placed the order for our meals in the bar and, after a short while, were escorted into the restaurant. We took our time over the dinner and enjoyed each other's company. Sarah had a lovely laugh and a gentle nature, making the evening a very pleasurable one. Afterwards, we sat together in the gazebo, where we had coffee and chocolates. During the evening, I could not help thinking about Carol and, inevitably, comparing the two women. Carol had more charisma and sexuality than Sarah, but was probably more emotionally unstable. It amused me to realise that

Carol was the closest to a nymphomaniac I was ever likely to have a relationship with.

When the time came for Sarah to leave, I walked with her to the car park. The evening had passed far too quickly and I was sorry she would have to leave. I asked if I could kiss her and she seemed quite happy to let me. I held her close and kissed her tenderly and yet with a hint of passion. She responded well and I felt her body give that little shiver of excitement as my lips teased hers. It was this familiar shiver which had led to my intimate relationship with Carol twelve months earlier and, I hoped, perhaps might lead to greater things with Sarah.

It was sad that we had to part when we were getting on so well, but we could not stay in the car park all night. "I'm sorry, John, but I'll have to go now. Thanks for a lovely evening. I'll phone you."

I wished her a goodnight and watched as her car drove away from the hotel. Slowly, I made my way back to my room. How I wished she would have stayed the night, but I knew that I was expecting too much of her. Apart from anything else, she would have had to pass reception to get to my room and this would have probably caused her most embarrassment. As I lay in my bed, I imagined the possibilities of what could have happened.

My fantasies ranged from making wild, passionate love to Sarah in the back of her car to slipping, naked, into the hotel's swimming pool, where we could again enjoy each other's bodies. With these images in my mind, I fell into a comfortable sleep, making do with the fantasy since the reality had not been possible.

Early next morning, I made my way to the leisure centre, eager to use the pool before it became busy. For about thirty minutes, I had the pool to myself. A woman and two noisy children disturbed my peace, giving me reason to leave the pool. Once I was dry, I thought I would try the apparatus in the gym, since I was now familiar with the layout. One of the machines particularly attracted me. It was the type where one kneels, while grasping the handles of a long bar with both hands raised above the head. The idea is to pull the bar downwards until it touches the back of the neck. This is intended to strengthen arm and shoulder muscles and, on the previous day, I had managed it quite successfully. This time, though, it was my legs which moved upwards, while the bar remained static. Apparently, the attendant had reduced the tension to a manageable level, the previous day. Now, I was exercising with the settings adjusted for the hunks who were obviously far more fit than me. Feeling a little ashamed of my lack of physical prowess, I had to reduce the tension on all the apparatus before I could use them.

I returned to my room, dressed properly for breakfast and made my way to the restaurant, ready and hungry for a full, English breakfast. Later that morning, I telephoned Kate to let her know that I was ready to leave when she was able to come. She said she would leave shortly and, with an impish laugh, asked if I would go along with a little joke of hers. I readily agreed and lazily lounged on my bed while she headed my car back towards Knutsford.

The telephone at the side of my bed rang and a rather bemused voice said, "Mr. Raynor, this is reception. Your driver is here."

Putting on my most imperious voice, I replied, "Oh, thank you. Could you send her along to my room, please?"

Two minutes later, there was a knock at my door. As I opened it, a giggling Kate entered my room. I collapsed with laughter at the sight of her. She was dressed in a black, trouser suit with white shirt and knee length leather boots. The only thing missing was the chauffeur's hat, but she had been unable to find one. Kate had a drink of tea in my room, made certain I had not left anything and then we went to reception to check out. To add to the effect, Kate carried my case for me. We had difficulty keeping a straight face as the receptionist prepared my invoice and presented it to me. Of course, I had to ask Kate to check it, but we felt certain the young woman behind the desk was suitably impressed.

Kate was always good company and I enjoyed the journey back with her. She stayed for a little while at my house and then returned to her own home. Late afternoon, I phoned Carol, hoping she would be back from her sister's. She was, and seemed pleased to hear from me. I told her about my hotel stay and date with Sarah. It always seemed strange that Carol and I should describe our dates with other partners.

It was she who phoned me, late that evening. Once again, she seemed to be coming closer to me. Nothing was ever certain with Carol, though, and, over the next few days, she still fluctuated between an intimate closeness and indifference, during our telephone conversations. It was a great relief when she agreed to come to my house on the following Saturday afternoon.

When my phone rang late Saturday morning, my heart sank as memories of previous cancelled arrangements flooded back. It was Carol. Sensing my apprehension, she quickly said, "Don't worry, love - I'm still coming. I just feel so low that I had to talk to you." The tears started to flow as she poured out to me all her fears, anxieties and troubles. With patience and careful reasoning, I managed to pacify her.

By far her biggest fear was that of being left on her own for the rest of her life. Although she admitted her love for me, Carol was adamant that she could not marry me. Only when she met the man who created the special feeling in her, would she marry. She was convinced that she would know this feeling when it happened. The trouble was, that Carol felt equally convinced that she was never going to find this elusive potential husband. At forty five years old, she knew that the chances of achieving happiness were difficult and getting less with each successive year. Eventually, when she felt able to continue her day without further comforting, we ended our conversation. Although I did not say as much, I did feel that her insecurity was well founded. I knew Carol was looking for something that did not exist. Equally, I felt that, in me, she had become closer to her ideal, than she was ever likely to with anybody else. If only she would compromise a little, I could have made her happy.

That afternoon, I had only just started to prepare for going out with Carol when the door bell rang. In her current troubled state, Carol had wanted to be with me and had arrived long before I expected her. I was wearing only my housecoat as I let her in. She closed the door and clung tightly to me, burrowing her head into my shoulder as she sobbed. I let her pour out the anxieties to me, yet again, as I tried to comfort her. Eventually, I was able to shower and dress, while Carol watched and talked to me. She did seem to have a fascination in watching me. I think she was constantly surprised that I was still able to perform normal tasks, despite my visual handicap, although she did observe that I did 'feel' for objects that a normally sighted person would locate precisely.

At last, I was ready and we drove, in my car, into the centre of Manchester. I had booked seats at the Royal Exchange theatre to see Arthur Miller's 'View from a Bridge'.

We both found watching plays in this 'theatre in the round' an unusual and pleasurable experience. After the show, we had a meal in a restaurant high up and overlooking Piccadilly Gardens. Carol seemed quite happy as we ate our meal, but I could sense a feeling of uneasiness in her. I knew Carol well enough by now to know that, no matter what I said or did, it would make no difference. We had been seeing each other for just a year and, in that time, we had become so close, we could almost read each other's minds. It was obvious, that day, that sex was the last thing on her mind and I should not expect her to satisfy my physical needs on this date.

We enjoyed the meal, but were disappointed to find the service painfully slow. This was mainly caused by two large groups of people having parties, that night. All the waiters were busily fussing around their tables, attending to their needs and neglecting ours. When the waiter never arrived to take the order for our sweet or coffee, we decided not to wait. I paid the bill, told the head waiter of our disappointment and left the Piccadilly hotel.

We did have coffee on returning home, but Carol left far earlier than I had wanted. We had just eight, lovely hours together. How

I hoped she would stay overnight, but I did realise that it would be impossible to change her mind, particularly on that day. In her mind, I had served the purpose of providing company and support for a few hours. It never seemed to cross her thoughts that I needed love and affection as much as her. Carol's way of providing beautiful, exotic love-making was almost like a mother giving sweets to a child for being good.

She would have been better to stay with me overnight, since she phoned and woke me up shortly after five, the following morning. Carol was in tears again and needed a lot of comforting. We talked for nearly an hour, when I suggested she should try to get some more sleep. She agreed and we both tried to fall asleep in our separate beds, but without success. Beds which were separated by more than fifty lonely miles and connected only by a fragile telephone cable. A little before eight o'clock, I decided to phone Carol. Like me, she had been unable to sleep, so we talked again for a while until it was time to get up.

During these lengthy telephone conversations, she told me many of her closest, most intimate secrets. Secrets of her past marriage and relationships. I could understand why she was so insecure when she told me of the things her ex-husband had done to her. Until now, she had kept these awful secrets to herself, but, in me, she had found someone she trusted enough to share them with. Her very early morning call was repeated again the next day, though we could not talk for as long since it was a Monday morning.

CHAPTER FOURTEEN - MAY, 1992

Carol's telephonic cry for help would not be possible for the remainder of that week, since she was to be one of the supervisors of her schoolchildren on an expedition. It seemed so strange for those few days to have no contact at all with her. I had hoped that she may be able to give me an occasional call just to keep in touch, but my phone remained ominously silent. The reason she gave was that, in the evening, the phone was heavily used by the schoolchildren calling their parents. She had phoned her own children, though, and I felt hurt that she had not thought it necessary to call me. Just a few words were all I had hoped for. Nothing that would make it obvious to the other teachers or children that she was talking to her lover.

Even after her return, she was so exhausted by the school expedition that she did not want to talk for long. I had to wait yet another week before I could see her again. Kate, my ex-secretary, had offered to drive me to Carol's when I wanted. It was a compromise, but a very welcome one. It did mean that I could travel the fifty miles in relative comfort, without worrying about trains or taxis. The main drawback was that Kate had to hang around until I was ready to return home.

When we arrived in North Wales on Monday, the May Bank Holiday, Carol suggested that we drive to Rhyl and politely asked Kate if she wanted to join us. Kate, diplomatically, declined and said she would just go for a walk in the area. Carol had become quite used to driving my car by now and headed towards the coast. It was a cool, windy day and the walk along the seafront was quite bracing, but not as warm as I had hoped. The weather was not good enough to stay for long and we soon returned to my car. There, we kissed a little, but Carol was obviously uneasy. She seemed in constant fear of being recognised even though we were not doing anything morally wrong. When I remembered how hot and passionate she had been in a car park in the middle of Chester, almost twelve months earlier, her present unease was a sharp contrast. We drove back to her house, where she made sandwiches and a drink for us all. The two women seemed to get on all right, but I felt certain that it was due more to politeness than anything else. Kate had told me long ago that I should have finished with Carol when she saw how much I was being hurt by our turbulent relationship.

Kate drove me home after what seemed such a frustrating day. I had felt deprived of any proper love or affection through Carol's misplaced 'mistress syndrome'. Still, I had, at least, seen her for a few hours.

Over the next few days, Carol returned to phoning me early morning, feeling quite depressed. She expressed a lot of anger when she was talking about Dave and I felt certain that reconciliation with him was now very unlikely. I felt that she had achieved a new landmark when she told me that she was going to tell the children that they would never see Dave again.

Much to my dismay, she did not want me to see her the following weekend. In a later telephone conversation, she apologised to me for constantly letting me down and hurting me. At times, she felt so depressed that she said things which she later regretted. Carol did lift my spirits when she declared that I was the best, closest friend she had ever known in her life. This uplift was short lived when she again declared that she could never marry me or even live together. Carol's variability was emphasised just a few days later when she told me how much she loved me and even talked of living with me.

After the fiasco of the holiday with Carol which never

materialised, I knew that, if I wanted to go away, the only thing to do was to book one for myself. With the pleasant memories of my Paris holiday in the spring of ninety one, I felt that May was again a good time to get away. This year, I decided that I should go to Amsterdam and had booked my flight and hotel early April. Since one of the most successful parts of my Paris holiday had been the day when I had a personal courier, I knew that I must organise the same thing again. This time, though, I was not going to wait until I was in the country before looking for a courier.

I telephoned the hotel in Amsterdam where I would be staying and asked to speak to the concierge. When I explained my situation, he provided me with the telephone number of a tourist travel centre. When I dialled the number, a woman speaking perfect English answered. I told her of my poor eyesight and asked if she knew of a woman who could act as my personal courier. I emphasised the 'woman' just to make certain that I did not end up being guided by a man. That was the last thing I would want. To my relief, she said she had the perfect person. A friendly, energetic woman with a bubbly personality sounded fine to me. She would have to speak with her first, to check if she would be available and interested. When I received a fax confirmation of the courier arrangements, I felt thrilled at having managed it so easily. There was a name and telephone number of the guide. I telephoned Mirz Braams, as she was called, and explained the situation to her. She had a lovely voice, pleasant manner and spoke excellent English. I arranged to meet her at my hotel at twelve thirty on Thursday, the fourteenth day of May.

To make certain that I did not oversleep on the day of my departure, I had booked an early morning call with British Telecom for a quarter to five. The night before, I had gone to bed early and phoned Carol. She seemed envious that I was going away and I knew that we would both miss each other. I promised to phone her whenever I could.

The taxi arrived at my house at six and drove me the short journey to Manchester Airport. As usual, the escorts there were superbly helpful and made certain that I boarded the correct flight. I know the other passengers must have been curious as to why I should receive preferential treatment in being escorted on to the plane before anybody else. My friends had always told me that, to a casual observer, there did not appear to be anything wrong with my eyesight, so there were bound to be some puzzled looks. I would still have preferred to be normally sighted, but I had to make the best of what little vision I did have.

The flight itself, though delayed for an hour, was quite short and uneventful. I was worried about being late for my appointment with Mirz. At Schiphol airport, I was provided with an escort to help me through customs and luggage collection. I was even helped to the rail station from the airport. My escort spoke to the guard on the train and asked him to make certain that I alighted at the correct station. He not only did that, but also found a porter who was to escort me directly to my hotel. The hotel was only a few minutes walk from the station, but I could not help wondering what British Rail would have done under similar circumstances. I was already impressed by the Dutch efficiency and friendliness.

My worst fears about the traffic in Amsterdam were realised as he assisted me in crossing the wide roads which separated the station approach from my hotel. The road was busy with cars, lorries, trams and hundreds of bicycles. There would be no way that I could safely walk through this busy city on my own and I was relieved that I had organised a personal escort. At the hotel reception, I thanked the porter and gave him a tip for his effort. The receptionist filled in the registration details for me and then found someone to show me the room. It was comfortable, but the view from my window was terrible. It looked into an inner area, with other buildings opposite and adjacent to my window. Since my room was only on the second floor of something like an eight storey building, the amount of light reaching my bedroom was minimal.

I soon realised that, if I wanted to find out what the weather was really like, I would have to leave the hotel. I supposed that the staff thought a view would be unnecessary bearing in mind, my reduced vision. In truth, it was just as important for me as for anyone else, since the character of the room becomes much more pleasant with the aid of natural sunlight.

It did disappoint me, since I had chosen this hotel because it was part of the same Skandik group as the most luxurious hotel I had ever stayed at in the centre of Stockholm. I did not have time to complain, just then, as I only had thirty minutes before meeting Mirz and I had yet to shower and change. I was just about ready, when the phone rang to announce her arrival in reception. With a final check on my appearance, I walked down the few flights of stairs and looked around.

A woman approached me. "Mr. Raynor?"

"Yes - are you Mirz?" I asked, a little nervously. I felt very pleased at the travel centre's choice. Mirz was a very slim, attractive woman about five foot four tall and probably in her mid thirties. I was soon to find that she had a delightful personality and I felt completely relaxed in her presence.

The brief I gave her was that I wanted to discover all I could about the real Amsterdam, not just the usual tourist stops. I knew that, if I had booked a package holiday, I would have missed a lot of the real character of the city. This delighted her as it was such a change from the usual requests. Before we moved very far from the hotel, we had to decide on the best way for her to guide me. I explained that, with my restricted vision, I missed a lot of detail and would need help to avoid colliding with or tripping over obstacles. She had never been faced with this situation before, but soon worked out the best approach.

Mirz proposed a different method from that of Carol's, but it actually turned out to be much better, giving an impression of me leading her, rather than being led. She walked on my left, with her shoulder just behind mine and our arms linked. Anyone seeing us, would have thought that we were just a courting couple with me leading her, but, in reality, she was guiding me with subtle movements of her hand and arm. As we were physically so close, I also felt the feedback from her body, such as when we went up or down kerbs. She supplemented this with quietly spoken information, making the whole process of getting around Amsterdam look so natural. I have never liked my handicap to be noticeable and Mirz had provided the perfect solution.

We walked for a while, until we reached a quiet, little restaurant, where we could have a drink while sitting overlooking one of the many canals. There, we talked happily, finding out much more about each other. It soon became obvious that Mirz was a very honest, open person. She asked many direct questions of me, which I had no hesitation in answering. She even asked my age which, though I do not like to admit just how old I am, I freely told her. In return, she told me her own age, which surprised me because she was older than her looks suggested.

I had not intended to, but I told her of my relationship with Carol and the problems she had caused me. Like my secretaries, Kate and Birgit, she felt that I was being taken advantage of and should end the relationship before I was hurt any more. I knew they were both right, but could not tear myself away from Carol. It was like a fatal attraction. After our drink, we walked further around the area, helping to build up a map in my mind. Within the space of a few hours of meeting, we had come to know each other well and felt very comfortable together.

I found Amsterdam to be a fascinating city. A city of many contrasts. Within a relatively short distance, there were busy shopping areas, tourist attractions, waterside walks and even semi-rural areas. Mirz showed me one of her favourite haunts, the Maritime Museum. She promised to show me round the place fully, but, on our first day, we settled for just a brief glimpse. This would give us more time for a general tour of the city to get a better idea of the geography.

It was fortunate that Mirz was able to spend the evening with me. After all our walking, we were quite hungry and I was happy to take her advice on choice of somewhere to eat. She knew of a Portuguese Restaurant which was in an area not bothered by tourists, where we had a lovely meal. This, to my mind, was the perfect way to spend a holiday. An interesting place, good weather and excellent company were to make this holiday one of the best I had ever known.

During our meal, we learned even more about each other. I was amazed to discover that Mirz could speak English, French, German, Spanish, Portuguese and Swedish as well as her native Dutch. I felt quite ashamed that I could only speak one of her seven languages, though I do know a little of the German language.

After the meal, she walked back with me to my hotel, telling me along the way about some of the people we were passing. There were some obviously on drugs and the occasional person asking for money, but, generally, we did not feel threatened or intimidated. Such people would be in evidence in most major cities throughout the world. I thanked her for a lovely day and asked her to take care in returning to her home.

Although it was only about ten thirty, I did feel quite tired and undressed for bed. As soon as I was in bed, I phoned Carol to tell her of my enjoyable day and new friend. She did seem pleased that I was having a good time and did not show any signs of jealousy when I told her about Mirz. Mindful of the expense of such a long distance call, we talked for only about ten minutes.

The next day, I had arranged to meet Mirz at twelve thirty and spent the morning quite lazily in my room. With all the potential dangers of exploring outside the hotel on my own, I felt determined not to take any chances and waited patiently for Mirz. That afternoon, we explored some other areas of Amsterdam and did a little shopping for presents. Her local knowledge proved to be invaluable for such purposes. To my surprise, Mirz invited me to her home and offered to make a meal for me. I was so pleased that she had accepted me as a friend and was intrigued to see what her place was like. It was, without doubt, the most unusual home I had ever entered and personified the unique nature of this very likeable woman. She had been living there for seventeen years and had originally moved into the place when it was a vacant butcher's shop.

A tiny porch led into what had been the front area of the shop, but was now her dining area. It was one large, through room with both kitchen area and lounge towards the rear. It was a very busy room and had a large part of one side wall covered with smart-looking shelving from floor to almost ceiling level. These shelves were stacked with many hundreds of books of a diverse nature and multitude of languages. There was no doubt about it; Mirz was a very well read woman.

A corridor from the back of this main room led to a toilet and shower. Although she had made a superb job of transforming a shop into a practical home, there were no obvious signs of luxuries. The income from her job did not leave much spare cash when she had paid for living expenses and food. Her sole living companion was Agnulta, an elderly cat, to which she was obviously devoted. The cat looked with curiosity at this new visitor and then came closer so as to brush past me. Apparently, according to Mirz, this meant that Agnulta approved of me.

After an enjoyable meal, Mirz said she would introduce me to some of her friends during our walk back to my hotel. These friends turned out to be a group of chickens and a pig. She had brought some food with her to feed the animals and it was obvious that the undemanding, uncomplicated affection of these creatures held a lot of attraction for her. To me, the fact that animals lived so close to the busy streets and waterways of Amsterdam, typified the unusual nature of this city.

The next day, Saturday, Mirz and I travelled by both tram and ferry allowing us to explore more distant parts of the city. We walked through a large park and sat for a while, watching people pass by. Since they weren't close enough for me to see them very clearly, Mirz described the people in great detail. Many rode past on bicycles, some pulling trailers with small children inside, clutching tightly. Whole families seemed to be riding through the park together, a far healthier approach to travel than the average British family.

This was the day when Mirz wanted to show me around her favourite place, the Maritime Museum. She was very patient and read many of the information panels on the exhibits and described those features which were difficult for me to make out. A full sized sailing ship was moored near to the museum and we spent a while looking around it.

Although it was not an area of Amsterdam which she liked, Mirz felt that I should see what the 'red light district' was like. As we walked through this area, she hung on tightly to me, protecting me from the women who were attempting to usher customers into the sex parlours.

The area struck me as unpleasant and rather squalid and not one to which I would wish to return. My eyesight was not good enough to see the scantily clad women posing in the shop-like windows of these brothels, though I did not feel too disappointed by this. We suspected that the majority of men in this area were more likely to be onlookers rather than potential customers.

We went vegetarian, that night, dining in a little restaurant, again away from the haunts of tourists. It was such an advantage to have the benefit of Mirz's local knowledge. She was continuing to act as my guide purely out of friendship, since my funds were only sufficient to cover her costs for the first two days of my holiday. I now felt very fond of her, but respected her friendship too much to jeopardise it by making what may have been an unwelcome pass at her.

When she escorted me back to my hotel, late in the evening, we would give each other a traditional Dutch gesture on parting - a kiss on each cheek. I hoped that I could remain friends with her for many years to come and, as with anybody who I considered to be a true friend, I would do anything I could to help her, no matter what she asked.

Carol was never very far away in my thoughts and, as soon as I was in bed, I telephoned her and talked for a few minutes. I think

I actually detected some signs of jealousy in her at the thought of me spending so much time with another woman, even though I assured her that it was an innocent friendship.

Sunday was to be my last full day in Amsterdam, but I would not be able to see Mirz until late afternoon. She was taking a party of tourists that day, but said she would be at my hotel as soon as possible. After breakfast, I visited the leisure centre and found that nobody was using the swimming pool. For over an hour, I was able to enjoy practising my swimming skills, without being hindered by other bodies. I found this to be the most comfortable pool I had yet tried, due mainly to the fact that Its depth was constant at one and a half metres. It was only after I finished my swim that I discovered the hotel had a massage service. I was unable to sample this, though, since I would have needed to book well in advance. I was disappointed that I was unable to compare the Dutch massage with those I had previously experienced. I felt pretty certain that it would not be as stimulating, in the full sense of the word, as that given by Jasmine in Singapore's Oriental Hotel.

I did ask to see someone from the hotel management so that I could show them how little natural light was available in my room. The man who came agreed with my observation and gave his apology. I did not really expect anything done about it, but I explained how the standard did not match that of the group's prestige hotel in Stockholm. He explained that my room was in the original part of the hotel and was due for major renovation work. He did show me the hotel's new block, where I found the standard to be much better.

It was after four in the afternoon when Mirz was able to come to my hotel. We weaved our way through the endless traffic towards the rail station and caught a train to Zentvoord on the coast. It was a lovely, hot, sunny May day as we walked together along the seafront. Mirz knew of a little shop serving traditional Dutch ice cream, an indication of its popularity being the length of the queue of people waiting to be served. It was a rich, creamy ice cream well worth waiting for.

After walking for a while through this pleasant seaside resort, we caught the train back to Amsterdam and looked for a suitable restaurant. This evening, our choice was for Italian food and Mirz found yet another superb place to eat. She was completely unpretentious and avoided expensive, over-rated restaurants, much to my relief. I knew, as we returned to my hotel, that, sadly, we did not have much more time together. She did stay for a little while and had a drink with me in the hotel bar. Sensing my sorrow at our impending separation she allowed me to hold her hand. With this simple gesture, I always felt able to communicate at a deep, yet non-sexual level with someone. I knew that, as a person, Mirz was far superior to Carol and yet, my heart was inextricably tied to Carol's. I did understand Mirz's preference for good, close, long-lasting friendships to brief, intimate relationships. Ultimately, they had to be more satisfying and rewarding. Another feature I liked about her was the way she did not look upon me as a handicapped person. She showed respect and understanding for me just as a normal man, which meant so much to me.

When we finished our drinks, she walked with me to the bottom of the stairs leading to my room. There, we held each other close and kissed on the cheek. As our heads moved to kiss on the other cheek, we stopped and kissed full on the lips. A soft, lingering, tender kiss. I wished it could have lasted longer, but the time had come to part. My eyes moistened with emotion as I said, "I do hope that we can see each other again. You're welcome to come and stay at my house whenever you like. Just let me know when you want to come." She thanked me and promised to keep in touch. I watched as she left the hotel before I went upstairs to my room.

I had to leave the hotel shortly after eight, the following morning for the flight back to Manchester and, with the usual help of airport staff, had a trouble-free journey back to Manchester. The anti-climax of returning home after such a good holiday hit me, yet again, as I unpacked my case and returned to normal everyday life. When I was certain that Carol would be home from school, I called her to let her know that I had arrived safely. We only talked for a few minutes, at that time, but it was later that evening when I spoke to her again, that she surprised me.

She admitted to me that she had been seeing another man over the last two weeks. I think she only told me then, because she had decided that he was not her type and had now finished with him. My mind was filled with jealousy at the thought of her being with another man and, yet, was I being hypocritical when I had just spent four wonderful days with another woman? There were differences which I felt certain justified my jealous feelings. Carol, by her own admission, had been seeking a potential marriage partner. In my case, I had, purely by chance, found a good friend in Mirz, but she had let me know that she had no intention of marrying and was not seeking an intimate relationship.

The fact that this other man had lasted less than a fortnight compared to our thirteen month relationship did provide some consolation. To be honest with myself, I did not mind Carol being friendly with other men, as long as she was not as intimate with them as with me.

The dependence Carol placed upon me was again very evident the next day. The phone at the side of my bed rang shortly after five in the morning, waking me with a start. Carol was feeling very low and was in tears. She knew that I would never be angry with her for disturbing my sleep and wanted to hear my calming voice. In that one day, she telephoned me five times and spent over two and a half hours talking to me. During one of those calls, she was practically hysterical because, on top of everything else, she was having trouble with one of her children. If only she would have let me marry her or even just live together, I felt certain that I could have solved her problems, but, as long as she resisted this logic, all I could do was listen and console her.

This pattern of calls was almost repeated the next day and, by this time, Carol's eyes were very sore through all her crying. Even the smallest incident, when combined with everything else, seemed a monumental problem to her and it was only by discussing it with me that everything could be put into its true perspective. By the end of the week, she was feeling much better and, to my relief, we were due to see each other on Saturday.

I had heard on the radio that there was a exhibition of Classic Cars at the National Exhibition Centre in Birmingham, and suggested that we went to it. Apart from the fact that I would enjoy it myself, I suggested it as something that would also interest her children. Travelling to an event like that as a family unit should help stabilise her relationship with the children and it would also give me an opportunity to get more used to them. Carol's response to my suggestion was good, but I was disappointed at the way she said it. "Yes, I'll take you there, John, if you would like me to."

"I don't want you to 'take' me anywhere", I replied in a hurt, rather than annoyed, tone. "I would like us to go together as a couple and nothing less."

"I'm sorry, John, I was not thinking." I accepted her apology and wondered if I was being too sensitive. Being treated as an invalid, was something I hated and it was not the first time I needed to remind Carol that I was just a normal man who desperately wished I could drive, but that would never be possible.

I had underestimated the problems she was experiencing with the children, since they refused to go with us and preferred to stay at home. Many women, faced with a similar situation, would have abandoned the trip completely, but Carol was determined that she and I should enjoy ourselves.

She arrived just before ten on the Saturday morning. She seemed so pleased to see me and it was very obvious that she was in a passionate mood. I was so relieved that her children had chosen not to come with us as we hurriedly stripped off and vigorously enjoyed each other's body. Carol seemed so hot and wild that morning and did not want to spend much time in foreplay, preferring to have me inside her in a frenzy of passion.

When we had satisfied our sexual desires, we dressed and set off on the road to Birmingham. It was a pleasant, sunny day and, with tapes of Carol's favourite singer, Tina Turner entertaining us, the journey seemed to pass quite quickly. There were many memorable cars of the fifties and sixties at the exhibition. Cars such as the mini, Jaguar 'E' types, Ford Anglia, MG sports cars and many others reminiscent of our youth. Of those cars which were for sale, the one which Carol would really have loved to own was a Jensen Interceptor costing a mere twenty nine thousand pounds. Other notable cars on display were Hitler's Mercedes and even the car in which John F. Kennedy was riding when he was assassinated. Carol did read to me many of the information plaques, describing the history of the cars. We both enjoyed the exhibition and stayed until late afternoon.

From Birmingham, we drove back northwards, this time heading towards Carol's house. When we did arrive, both of us felt hot and sticky and decided to have a shower. Since Carol's children were there, we had to behave ourselves and showered separately. Later on, all four of us went to an Italian restaurant. I so wanted to make good friends with the boys that I was anxious about their reaction to me. I need not have worried as the whole occasion went very smoothly and Carol and I were able to give unseen reassuring little squeezes on our side of the table. She did tell me, later on, that both boys behaved far better with me than they had ever done with Dave. I supposed that this was understandable, since they would have seen Dave as the man behind their parent's divorce.

Even though we had spent the whole of that evening as a family, Carol still dare not let me stay at her house overnight and had booked me into a local hotel. I could never understand why she insisted on hiding the fact that we were lovers and had been so for over twelve months. It was almost as though she was ashamed of her feelings for me. I listened to many of the programmes on Radio One and it was quite obvious from what people said when phoning in, that many couples were living together without shame. If a woman phoned the Simon Mayo quiz at a quarter to seven in the morning and referred to her boy friend being in the same room, Simon invariably would remark jokingly, "Oh, I see - your boy friend just came round to make certain you're okay." One day, hopefully, I would be accepted fully into this family.

Carol drove me to my hotel, had a look at my room, which was fairly basic, and then returned to her house. At eight thirty, the next morning, she came back to my hotel and had breakfast with me, which, to me, seemed a nice gesture. We drove the short distance back to her house, where I was to spend a lazy morning, apart from helping with the preparation of the Sunday lunch.

Carol had arranged to go to aerobics with her friend, Barbara, during the morning and left me in her house with the boys. When Barbara arrived, she sounded the car horn as a signal to Carol. This was to be the day, or so I thought, when I would meet Barbara on their return from aerobics. I had heard so much about her that I was looking forward to the meeting, but I was to be disappointed. She just dropped Carol off and drove away, an indication to me that Carol had either made some excuse for us not meeting, or, perhaps, had not even told Barbara of my presence. It was almost as though she was afraid of me getting too close to her family and friends. I tried not to let my disappointment show and chatted to Carol in the kitchen as she finished preparations for our meal. Every so often, we would steal a kiss, when the boys were not around. It was a lovely, hot May day and we were able to enjoy our meal, sitting around the table on the patio.

I was yet to discover that this afternoon was to be one of the most unusual and stimulating ones of my life. Shortly before three, Carol and I began to prepare for the journey back to my house. As I was leaving the bathroom, where Carol had just been checking my weight, she enticingly invited me into her bedroom. How I wished we could have made love there and then. We did kiss and I fondled her breasts. Her sighs on feeling my fingers touching her gently were an indication of just how sexually hot she was that day. I could see an erotic thought filling her mind, as she said, "I know! I'll just wear a tee shirt without my bra and then you can touch me all the way to your home."

"Mmmm.. I like the sound of that." My sexual arousal increased as I watched her changing her jeans and slipping on a light tee shirt. I said goodbye to the boys and excitedly climbed into Carol's car. We waited until we were a couple of miles away from her house and then I slid my hand inside her tee shirt. Her nipples were large and erect as I fondled and caressed her breasts.

Initially, the idea was to take the longer, country route home, but we both became so sexually aroused, that we changed our minds and took the motorway instead. I would have made love to her in a quiet, country lane, but Carol preferred to wait until we reached my home and the comfort of my bed, rather than the confines of a Peugeot 203. As I teased her nipples, she was obviously deriving superb pleasure from my actions. The fact that we were travelling at around seventy miles an hour on the motorway, did not seem to bother her and she kept good control of the car as I continued caressing her. In retrospect, I would not recommend any couples to indulge in such foreplay on the motorway, as we were fortunate not to have a collision. I also wondered if other drivers could tell just what we were doing to each other.

At one point, when we were stopped at traffic lights, Carol pulled the top of her tee shirt away and looked down inside it to see just what I was doing with my hand. This simple action amused me as she seemed almost like a little girl curious about her own body. "Oh, John, I love it when you do that. It seems to have a direct link with here." She touched her pubic area. At times, my hand would descend to the top of her legs, when she would squeeze her thighs tightly, trapping my hand against this deeply sensitive area. As she realised how my penis was straining at the fabric of my trousers, she unzipped my fly and slipped her hand inside, gripping me tightly. This would help to maintain my erection and prevent premature ejaculation. We continued playing with each other in this highly erotic way for nearly an hour, until we pulled up outside my house. I am certain that we both must have been flushed with excitement as we hurriedly left the car and I tried, without success, to hide the obvious bulge in my trousers.

Once inside, we quickly stripped naked and started to make love in my living room. Carol had an orgasm there, but I was saving the best for the bedroom. We rushed upstairs and started full intercourse again on my bed. It was a powerful, very physical, almost violent performance with loud, orgasmic sighs from both of us. I realised afterwards that the bedroom window was open and my neighbours, sitting on their patio, probably heard us. It really did not matter as Carol and I had spent the most beautiful, erotic afternoon ever and one I would remember for the rest of my life. In fact, the whole weekend had been superb.

Unusually, she did not seem to be in a hurry to leave and stayed for a while as we held our sweating bodies close together. During the next hour, we made love several times, until we were both exhausted. Like all good things, it had to end at some time and, eventually Carol had to leave for home.

Not surprisingly, when I telephoned her late that night, she was very drowsy and could not stay awake for long. I let her slip into a comfortable, relaxed sleep. I felt that we were closer now than we had ever been and hoped the future would bring us even more close. During the next few days, she agreed that it had been a wonderful weekend, but, as if she could sense my ambition, again said she could never marry me. She insisted that we would not be able to see each other every weekend, so that she may still have a chance of meeting someone else.

Over the next week, she varied from telling me how much she loved me to feelings of guilt that she could not ever feel for me what she felt for Dave.

CHAPTER FIFTEEN - JUNE, 1992

Carol's sister and family were staying with her for a few days, which prevented us talking for long or seeing each other. It was a weekday, in the first week of June, when she phoned me at four thirty in the morning. She was having difficulty sleeping and wanted to talk to me to settle her mind a little. Eventually, she felt able to sleep again, but this was to be the start of a very traumatic day for Carol.

When I phoned her at eleven, that evening, it was Carol's son who answered. He told me that she had gone out and not yet returned. She would, normally, let me know if she was likely to be out until late and there had been no mention of it, that morning. My first thought, was that she was out seeing another man. I did have a strange, inexplicable feeling that this was not the case and felt quite worried for her safety.

I felt certain that she would ring me as soon as she arrived home, but could not just wait. Every twenty minutes, I dialled her number and just let it ring for four times, hopefully preventing her children from being disturbed. There was absolutely no way I could fall asleep under the circumstances and, as midnight passed without any call, my anxiety grew worse. She would never have stayed out so late when she would have to teach at school the following day. I knew, instinctively, something was seriously wrong and feared the worst. I prayed that she was alive and safe and hoped that it would not be long before I heard her voice again.

It was almost two o'clock before the phone rang and, by this time, I was feeling sick with worry. She was safe and uninjured, but had been involved in a car accident. It was a miracle she had escaped so lightly since her car was practically a write-off. Apparently she had been driving along a country lane, when a car coming in the opposite direction, had veered onto the wrong side of the road and collided head-on into Carol's car. The other driver had been drinking and had neither tax nor insurance.

Remarkably, she was quite calm, but admitted that she felt relieved at being able to tell me just what had happened. The police had taken statements from everyone involved and had brought Carol home. Even the police thought she had been very lucky to remain unscathed and I felt certain that a guardian angel must be looking after her. After talking for about half an hour, she felt that she might be able to sleep, but neither of us managed to get much rest, that night.

Understandably, she felt uneasy at driving after this accident and I would have understood if she had cancelled her date with me for the Saturday. I would have happily travelled to meet her to save her the journey, but she decided to come after all. She had managed to borrow a Mini for a few weeks until the extensive damage to her car had been repaired.

When she did arrive at my house on Saturday evening, we both felt so relieved to see each other and clung tightly together for a while. We left the Mini at my house and drove into Manchester in my SAAB. It was obvious that her confidence had suffered and it would be quite a while before her usual self-confidence would return. She accepted that, if she had not driven to see me, it would have taken even longer to return to normal.

I had booked a table at one of the hotels we frequently used in the centre of Manchester. During our meal, which was in the restaurant overlooking Piccadilly Gardens, she told me more about the accident and the drunken idiot who had caused it. At first, it was thought that her car was a write-off, but the garage decided they could repair it.

This evening, we were not going to the theatre at all, as we usually did, and drove back to my house after the meal. We relaxed and watched television for a while. It was obvious that the accident had unsettled Carol and sex was the last thing on her mind. Much as I would have wanted to make love, I respected her feelings and just provided companionship for her. Shortly before eleven, she left for home, leaving me wishing that I could have gone with her.

As if to emphasise Carol's variability, within a matter of days, she was talking, once again, of seeing Dave. She would make no promises of seeing me again, much to my disappointment. After all, it was me she phoned after her accident and it was me who always listened to her many problems and tried to help her. Dave had done nothing except waste several years of her life and, yet, he still had this magical hold over her. I found great difficulty sleeping properly for the next few nights as the woman I was so desperately in love with, discussed with me how strongly she felt for Dave. I advised her not to accept any compromises from him and only agree to stay with him if he would divorce his wife and marry Carol.

Whatever was happening between them must not have been going smoothly, as her calls to me became more frequent and, invariably, she would be in tears. Hour long calls during the early hours of the morning, when she would be seeking comfort from me, again became more commonplace. The number of calls from Carol was always a good indication of how close she was to me and, for the next two weeks, although we did not see each other, she phoned me a great deal. On many occasions, she did say that she loved me and told me that she had never been able to discuss her intimate thoughts and feelings with anybody else in the way we could.

When I pressed her as to why she would not marry me, she gave me a reason which hurt me so deeply, so painfully, that I wondered why I still loved this ruthless, selfish woman. She could never marry anyone with a handicap, such as my poor eyesight. It would be different, she reasoned, if I was to lose my eyesight after marriage to her, but she could not cope with marrying anyone with such a disability. I had become accustomed to people's natural prejudice to anything out of the ordinary, but knew that this was primarily due to ignorance. Carol, of all people, had known me for over a year and was very much aware how I did not let my poor vision be an obstacle to living a normal life. If only I had divorced three or four years earlier when I could see well enough to read, I might have been able to overcome such obstacles.

I knew, from this, that her so-called love for me must not be true love at all. I told her that my love for her was such that, even if she had a leg missing, I would still want her. I did realise that, probably the primary obstacle to her loving me fully was her need to feel the same as she did for Dave. It was extremely unlikely that she would ever find this feeling again with anyone, not even Dave.

As the school holidays were approaching, Carol was feeling somewhat depressed at the prospect of nearly two months at home. My first reaction was to offer to take her on holiday, but, from past experience, I had always been let down by Carol. It came as a surprise when she agreed to go away with me. Even then, I felt certain that she would change her mind before I had chance to arrange anything definite. My suggestion was that we should have three, short breaks spread throughout the holiday. This idea appealed to her and she left me to come up with some suggestions.

My sister ran a small hotel in a remote part of the Lake District and I had not, as yet, stayed there. Even though this would mean that her identity would become known to my family, Carol did not reject the idea and even thought it would be a good place to go.

When I spoke to Bob Platts, my brother-in-law to see if they had room at the hotel, the first question he asked was, "Is it for two single rooms?"

He had quite a reputation as a joker, but I still felt a little embarrassed as I replied, "No. Just a double room, please."

Being aware that Carol may yet change her mind, I did not make a definite booking, but gave him a provisional date. According to Carol, the only reservation she had was that I might feel uncomfortable at taking her to a place run by my relatives. It did not worry me at all and, in fact, was probably the only way I was likely to see the hotel. It was with great surprise and relief, therefore, that I was able to book our first holiday.

Meanwhile, I had also suggested that Carol, her children and I visit the Granada Studio Tour in Manchester. Again, she accepted this and it was arranged for the last Saturday in June. They arrived in the Mini, which she was still having to use, at about half past one. We decided to drive into Manchester in the SAAB, since it would be a lot more comfortable. Carol was a regular viewer of Coronation Street and was fascinated, as we all were, by the television sets. 'The Street' was a very dominant part of the tour, but the studios showing techniques for televising proved to be truly fascinating. We were able to sit in a replica of the House of Commons, in our case on the Opposition Benches, while a staged comic debate took place. All four of us enjoyed the afternoon and I felt relieved that the boys seemed to accept me as part of their family.

When we returned to my house, Carol made a meal and, afterwards, we left the boys watching television while the two of us walked to a local pub. There, we planned our holidays for the next two months. Carol was not a person to plan far ahead, but she did tell me how much she enjoyed organising our holidays. Even though we were closer now than we had ever been, she still would not let me go back with her and the boys to their house. As an alternative, I suggested that they all stay at my place instead, but that was not acceptable to her either. Once again, we were separated by Carol's misplaced shell of shame, and I watched as their car disappeared into the distance.

During our late-night telephone conversations, we talked more of our holidays. I felt that we were being unfair to her children in excluding them from our plans and suggested that we should all go together for one of our holidays. She was not very keen on the idea, but agreed that it would be unfair to exclude them. She was so worried about what they would think of her if they knew that she was sleeping with me, but eventually, accepted my suggestion. I had more opportunity to use the telephone and so, I offered to call travel agents and make all the bookings.

CHAPTER SIXTEEN - JULY, 1992

Despite the fact that we were now so close, Carol still felt that she should continue looking for a potential marriage partner and had booked to have a meal with members of a Dinner Circle. On the Saturday she was due to go for this meal, she phoned me early morning and talked for an hour and a half. She was having second thoughts about going for the meal and very nervous about the occasion. Although I wanted to keep her for myself, I knew that this was not only selfish but also impossible and convinced her that it was worth trying.

I spent a very anxious evening on my own while Carol tried this new social experience. I imagined all types of scenario, where Carol would meet an attractive man and, perhaps, go back to his place afterwards. She had done this with me, so why not with someone else? I could not concentrate on anything and went to bed at eleven thirty to await her phone call. There was no way I could fall asleep and my anxiety grew worse as time passed. Carol had expected to be home by midnight, but it was one thirty before she phoned. Apparently, it was shortly after midnight before she left the restaurant, but she had locked herself out of her house and had been trying to waken her son to let her in. As a last resort, she had to phone him and leave it ringing until it finally disturbed him.

There had been more women than men at the restaurant and none of the men had impressed her. Carol had made friends with a couple of women, but, to my relief, declared that she would not be going again. She knew how jealous I was of her wanting to meet someone else and always tried to re-assure me of the strength of her feelings for me.

I had been hoping to see Carol, the following weekend, but, in the middle of the week, she told me that she and the boys would be going to her sister's for the weekend. Yet again, she had let me down and at a time when we seemed to be so close. I also felt disappointed when she told me she had given the boys the impression that she was going on a course at the time we would be staying at my sister's. I could not understand why she had to tell so many unnecessary lies and felt sorry for the boys. Just what was she ashamed of? I felt certain that her children must realise that we were lovers and were responsible enough to be told the truth.

She did delight her boys by telling them about the holiday they would be taking with us. I had booked for us to go to Paris for five days and one of those days would be at Euro Disney. Their only regret was that it was not longer, preferably a fortnight. She was relieved that they had not asked any awkward questions about our relationship. Carol had even told her best friend, Barbara, about us which, to my mind, was a major breakthrough. She did ask me not to expect too much from her just because she was now being more open about our relationship.

Our first holiday started on a Friday in the middle of July. Carol arrived at my house about five thirty and transferred her luggage into my car. We did not waste much time and set off on the journey to the Lake District, with Carol now feeling quite used to driving my SAAB. It did not take long to cover the motorway part of the journey, but our progress became much slower once we were on the narrow, twisting country lanes. As we climbed ever higher up the bleak, yet beautiful, Cumbrian hills, the temperature dropped noticeably and a light mist surrounded us.

The car handled the steep, winding roads without complaint and Carol obviously enjoyed the challenge of such a journey. In the middle of nowhere and eleven hundred feet above sea-level, we finally found the High Windy Hall Hotel.

My sister, Pauline, greeted us and showed us around the building. She presented us with a difficult choice, by saying that we could have either of two rooms. One of them would be next to a young couple with a baby, while the other was adjacent to the room used by my sister and brother-in-law. I decided that the room next to my sister's would be preferable, since I did not want to be disturbed by a baby's crying. Carol did feel a little uneasy at being so close to my relatives as she felt they might be able to hear us while we were making love, but agreed it was the right choice. It was the first time I had seen the hotel and was impressed by the standards of the rooms. We had a Queen size double bed, of which we intended making good use. Carol was thrilled at the prospect of a relaxing, romantic weekend in such surroundings.

We quickly freshened up and went downstairs to the lounge, where we had a drink with Pauline, and ordered our meal. It was a typical family business and my nephew, Cameron, as chef, prepared an excellent meal. We took our time over the various courses and enjoyed a bottle of wine, both of us feeling very relaxed and comfortable. When we did eventually get to bed, we were a little tired, but this did not stop us from making love. As we were reaching our climax, Carol managed to restrain herself from being too vocal. I must have been noisier than I realised, since Carol put her hand over my mouth to silence me. It was lovely to be able to just fall asleep afterwards, with our naked bodies close together in the centre of the large bed.

When we awoke the next morning and opened the curtains, the view from our window was stunning. It was a brilliant, sunny day and we could see for miles over the lush, green valleys spread out below us. After a drink of tea, we returned to our bed and made beautiful love again.

In many ways, what we had was better than marriage, since it seemed like a new, exciting experience every time we made love. We constantly experimented in different positions while having sex, both of us being eager and willing to try almost anything. I particularly enjoyed the shallow angle penetration achieved by keeping her thighs close together. It produced a superb sensation which worked well for both of us. Carol did feel that she may blush with embarrassment when we entered the dining room for breakfast, as my sister would know what we had been doing. Since we were only doing what comes naturally to lovers, I felt certain that she had no need to be concerned and, in the event, she seemed to be alright.

After a good breakfast, we drove into Carlisle, had a wander around the shops and spent quite a while in the museum. Carol decided that she must buy a camera to record the beautiful scenery of the area. One of the disposable cameras proved ideal for the purpose and she took many shots from the hotel, capturing the spectacular, rural views. On our way back to the hotel, we stopped in a tiny village, which, judging from the many expensive cars lining the narrow, cobbled roads, had fallen victim to the invasion of tourists. It had not spoilt the village but it did seem to have a strange conflict of character. We found a lovely little shop which seemed to sell everything, especially some imitation orange poppies and a copper flower container, which Carol could not resist.

My brother-in-law, Bob, was at the hotel when we returned that night and gave us an enthusiastic welcome. With bow tie and smart waistcoat he looked the part as he played both host and head waiter in the restaurant. He was a barrister by profession, but seemed to enjoy the contrast, looking after guests in the hotel during the weekends. I think I upset his timing for our meal, as Carol and I were in deep conversation and took ages over our first course. Carol noticed that he kept looking anxiously at our table to see if we were ready for the next course.

We talked, as we did on many occasions, about us and our feelings for each other. It would have been obvious to anyone that I was deeply and hopelessly in love with Carol. She, on the other hand, had some reservations about our future, although she admitted that she did love me and felt superbly comfortable when we were together. The two principal hindrances to our romance were the strength of feeling she still had for Dave and her inability to accept my visual handicap. While we enjoyed our relationship, both emotionally and physically, neither of us knew how it may develop over the long term. Occasionally, I would take hold of her hand and let her feel the warmth of my love as I put my whole heart into this physical contact. We never did reach a solution, but were both determined to enjoy each other, at least for the remainder of our holidays.

Eventually, Bob was able to serve the main course, which was extremely enjoyable and, with a delightful dessert, easily satisfied our appetites.

Back in the privacy of our bedroom, we swiftly removed our clothes and held each other close and kissed, full on the lips. My lips then caressed her cheek and neck as they tantalisingly discovered other areas of arousal. When my mouth descended lower to her breasts and then engulfed her nipple, the familiar tingle of excitement ran through Carol's body. She pressed her pubic area hard against mine and gave long, arousing sighs of pleasure as the desire for intercourse intensified. She opened her legs and pulled me closer into her, giving a little cry of ecstasy as I entered. It was superb to make love to Carol as she responded so sensitively and, yet, energetically to my slow, firm thrusts. This time, somehow, we both managed to keep the noise level to one that should not have disturbed anyone else.

How I wished that this relationship, the best physical one I had ever experienced, could have lasted forever. That second, superb night in the Lake District, was the last one for this short holiday. We drove back leisurely the next day, travelling past lakes Ullswater and Windermere. Just before our holiday, Carol had said she would tell the boys the truth about where she was going, but, in the event, she found it impossible to admit that she had previously lied to them. I could understand her difficulty, but felt certain that the initial lie had been unnecessary. The only consolation at our parting was that there were two more holidays yet to come.

The biggest disappointment over the next few days was when I discovered that Dave had phoned and Carol had allowed him to go to her house. It always unsettled her when she had any contact with him and I desperately wished he would stay away. He was the proverbial 'bad penny' and one of the main hindrances to our continued relationship. Although it was a few days later before she let me know, Carol apparently told Dave of her intended Paris holiday.

When he asked if just she and the boys were going, she told him that I would also be there. I still do not know just how much she told him about me, but it must have come as quite a shock. How I wished I could have seen his face.

I was really pleased when Martin, Carol's younger son, phoned me and told me what places they would like to visit while in Paris. He asked me if I thought their plans would be alright. Although it was a simple gesture, it meant so much to me that he should seek my approval. I told him that it sounded great to me and I was so looking forward to the holiday. He sounded excited and told me that he had drawn some money out of his Building Society account to buy an Olympus camera. A few days later when I was talking to Carol late one night, Martin came on the phone and asked me what was likely to happen to his camera when we would be passing through Customs. He was worried that it may be stolen, lost or damaged, but I assured him that nothing was going to happen to it.

At last, the day of departure arrived. It was Thursday, the thirtieth day of July and quite a landmark in my life. I felt accepted as a part of another family, as we took a taxi to Manchester Airport for the thirteen twenty flight to Paris. Martin's camera survived Customs, much to his relief. I gave each of the boys a bag of sweets and a book of 'Odd Facts and Information' to relieve any boredom during the journey.

Of the four of us, it was Carol who was a little nervous about the flight. She did not like the sensation during ascent and descent, but felt much better once we had landed. We could have taken a bus journey from the airport to the centre of Paris, but that would have meant walking with our luggage in an unfamiliar area, looking for our hotel. I did not want anything to go wrong with this holiday and insisted that we take a taxi directly to the hotel. Carol's older boy, Peter, could speak a little French and acted as translator to the cab driver.

The hotel I had booked was only small, but very comfortable. It was just off the Champs Elysees and, I felt, a good position for our excursions. I was hoping that the boys' room would not have a connecting doorway to ours as this would not offer much privacy. To my relief, the layout was superb. A door from the hotel corridor led into a hallway, from which there were doors to our rooms. Better still, the boys' bathroom was sandwiched between the two bedrooms and that was one place they were unlikely to spend much time. Peter and Martin were pleased with their room, mainly because it had satellite television.

Carol loved our room and enthused over the luxurious bathroom, air conditioning and fridge full of drinks. Neither of us felt uncomfortable when the boys wandered into our room to see how it compared with theirs. The thing which pleased me most was the fact that we had a double bed, although this had not been guaranteed. In fact, it was two single beds pushed together, but with double size bedding.

It was late afternoon by the time we had settled in, so we did not travel much on our first day. Apart from going out for a meal, we mainly familiarised ourselves with the area. Although I longed to have sex, I did not insist on it for our first night, as Carol was still a bit apprehensive about the boys being so close. Peter and Martin did not seem very curious, but if I had been a boy under similar circumstances, I would have had my ear pressed to the wall, listening for those familiar bedroom noises. We seemed to sleep quite well and were happy just to cuddle up close.

A cruise along the river Seine was the main attraction on our itinerary for the next day. Martin, armed with his new camera, had plenty of opportunities for good shots, but was fairly economic in his choice of sights to record. There was a photographer on board the cruiser, taking photos of the passengers without asking if they were wanted. Carol intensely disliked having her picture taken and did not want to buy the print displayed as we stepped back on to dry land. When we had separated the previous June, I had asked for her photograph, but this was one thing she refused to do.

It was a lovely, sunny day and we all enjoyed discovering the attractions of Paris. Because of my poor vision, I felt useless at finding my way around and had to rely on Carol and Peter's map reading and limited French vocabulary. In the evening, we found a pleasant little restaurant in the Latin area for our meal. I felt so pleased that the boys were comfortable and at ease with me. Although they were a bit awkward with Carol on occasions, I knew that it would be wrong for me to discipline them since it would take time for me to adopt the role of their father.

Carol and I did make beautiful love, that night, with my excitement being heightened because of the situation we were in. The main concern was to keep our orgasmic vocals as quiet as possible. Once we were in the privacy of our own room, Carol lost any inhibitions and we enjoyed each other's body several times over the next few days.

CHAPTER SEVENTEEN - AUGUST, 1992

The following day, we visited the Louvre, where, because of all the unbalanced publicity, one might expect to find only one painting and one sculpture, namely the Mona Lisa and the Venus de Milo. Needless to say, there were many other fine exhibits, making the tour around the museum quite lengthy. Carol and I decided that we would like a meal on our own, that night, and suggested to the boys that they eat at MacDonald's. This suited them fine and allowed us to use the Metro to find a more sophisticated restaurant. The place we intended using was, surprisingly, closed, apparently because it was Saturday night, but we found another not far away, which proved to be very suitable. It amazed me that we were never short of things to say to each other and enjoyed the intimacy of this small restaurant and the French cuisine. As always, we each had different courses so we could share and feed each other.

Sunday, the last full day of our holiday, was meant to be especially for the boys. We travelled by R.E.R. to Euro Disney, the place which Martin had been particularly looking forward to. I had visited Disneyworld in Florida several years earlier and found the Paris equivalent much the same, but it still did not spoil my enjoyment. After a stimulating ride on Star Travel and the deafening spectacle of Michael Jackson's Captain Eo, Carol and I suggested that the boys continue on their own. We thought we might hinder them from going on what they wanted and arranged where we would meet again. It came as quite a surprise when we came across them only a few minutes later, queuing for the Mississippi Steamboat.

I thought they would have preferred something a little faster, but, as Carol said to me, “They seem to lack the spirit of adventure.” I felt then that they would probably enjoy themselves better if they stayed with us, so that we could make certain they did not miss anything. When I saw the Runaway Train racing up and down the island in the middle of the lake, I felt that it must be worth the experience. Carol was not too happy when I suggested going on this train, but agreed that it was probably the only way to get the boys to try it.

There was a long queue for this very popular ride, but, in fact, there was an even longer, unseen queue inside the boarding station. It took over three quarters of an hour to reach the point where we could actually get in the train. Carol sat next to me and the boys were in the carriage behind us, all held firmly in place by safety bars. The surroundings were meant to look like a mine and our group of carriages sank downwards into a dark tunnel. This clever feat of engineering then took us under the lake on which we had previously been sailing. When the train reached the island, it climbed slowly upwards inside the mountain. At the top, we emerged into the brilliant sunshine and were presented with a tremendous view. We did not get much chance to see it as the train shot down a steep track and round impossible-looking curves. It was a tremendous, exhilarating ride, with many passengers, including Carol, screaming. We held hands on the safety bar and enjoyed the occasion of being together as a family. Peter and Martin both thought the experience to be fantastic and happy that we had tried this superb ride.

The parade along Main Street seemed quite tame after that, but it was another fine example of the professionalism of Disney theme parks. Martin, apparently, talked endlessly about this day for many weeks to come.

On our last day in Paris, we were determined to travel right to the top of the Eiffel Tower. It was worth the long queue and the crush within the lifts. The view from the top, almost a fifth of a mile above the ground, was overwhelming and justification alone for Martin's investment in his new camera. It was a beautifully clear, sunny day and, even with my limited vision, I could appreciate the spectacle of Paris displayed in miniature all around us. Panoramic photographs were displayed all around the room at the top of the tower to allow the observer to identify landmarks.

The Pompidou Centre was the final attraction we were determined to see before leaving Paris and, although we did not have much time to look round the centre, we saw enough to get a feel of the place. The unusual architecture of this famous landmark, with escalators encased in glass tubes on the outside of the building, made it well worth a visit.

The flight home marked the end of yet another superb holiday. Although Carol had said several times that she wished we had gone without the boys, I felt it would have been unfair to leave them at home. Back at my house, they piled all their luggage in Carol's car, thanked me for taking them away and then, I was once more on my own as they drove away. The separation from Carol was even more painful on this occasion, as we had not left each other's side for the past five days. I wished it could have lasted for ever. I do not know how she did it, but Carol had the magical effect of making me feel like a million dollars whenever I was with her. I suppose it was a mixture of charisma, vulnerability, sensitivity and sensuality which gave her this power of attraction.

When Carol phoned me the next day, she gave me quite a shock. Dave had, apparently, phoned her that morning. Apart from asking if she had enjoyed her holiday, he actually agreed that their relationship could never work. Although he had only stated the obvious, she had been upset by him saying it. In a fit of pique, she had told him that she was getting married. Married! If only that were true. I realised then that she was now doing to Dave what she had done to me the previous June. She seemed to use her mythical act of marriage as a means of 'dumping' men who no longer served a purpose in her life.

Even Carol could not explain the reason for what she did next. About mid-morning, she drove a two hour journey to Dave's home, only to discover that he was not there. She had no idea what she would have said if he had been at home and, in some ways, felt relieved that her long drive had been a waste of time. She then returned home and was in tears for most of the journey. As if to seek approval of her actions, she called at Barbara's and told her what she had done. Apparently, Barbara told her that it was a very stupid thing to do and offered no sympathy. Since Carol did not want to phone during office hours, she waited until early evening before calling me. I did not offer her much sympathy either and felt quite upset that she had done such a crazy thing the very day after we had returned from our holiday. Unlike Barbara, I was prepared to listen and try to help her in understanding her strange actions.

Over the next few days, she phoned me early morning and several times during the day. Most of the times, as I answered the phone, she was already in tears and needed much comforting. The one boost she gave to my confidence during these difficult calls came when she said that I was worth four of Dave. She found that my moral strength and calm approach to helping her to be invaluable. On many occasions, we had agreed that, no matter what happened, we would stay in touch for the rest of our lives.

Even if this might not be possible, I decided to create a permanent reminder of our relationship. I found a photo specialist, where I could have any photograph enlarged and printed on a panel backing, making it appear like a large painting which could be hung on a wall. I felt that the photograph, taken by Carol's son, from the top of the Eiffel Tower, would be the most appropriate, bearing in mind how Carol disliked having her photo taken. I had two copies made and would present one to Carol and keep the other for me. I just hoped that she would not dispose of her copy, as this may be the only lasting memento of our time together. I remembered the sexy French knickers and the gold necklace with Jade pendant which I had also given her and, equally, hoped she would retain these items.

It was just over a week after returning from our holiday before I saw Carol again. It was Tuesday and my birthday. My secretary was on holiday that day and Carol had offered to act as my personal assistant for the day. She arrived at ten to nine and wanted to do everything that my secretary would normally do. First, she went through the post and read all the letters to me and, as usual, discarded a lot of junk mail. I had decided that we should do some programming and gave Carol directions on what she should type at the computer keyboard. She was a very willing pupil and soon became used to acting as my eyes. When the phone rang, she would answer it promptly in her most imposing secretarial manner.

She seemed to be enjoying herself and, as we were sitting next to each other at the computer, we would occasionally give each other a kiss. After we had some lunch, we went for a short walk around the area. It was when we returned and continued our programming that we digressed from what could be described as a fairly conventional day. Carol was sitting at the side of me when I put my arm around her waist. I gave her a loving squeeze and touched her breast with my other hand. She responded by taking my hand and putting it inside her jumper. As I caressed her, I could see that she was quickly becoming aroused.

"Let's go upstairs" she said as her need for me intensified.

"I'll put the answer phone on, so we won't be disturbed."

"No, don't do that. Just leave the phone so that we can still answer it."

I was surprised by her request, but let her have her way. I was praying that nobody would phone while we were in the middle of making love, but this possibility actually added to the excitement, as Carol had anticipated. There was a phone at the side of my bed, so I could have answered it if necessary, but probably would have been rather breathless. I closed my bedroom curtains and we both quickly stripped naked. She was already hot and moist and did not want to wait any longer for penetration.

"I love it when you're forceful, Darling. Do it hard to me." I happily obliged and put all my energy into a very physical manifestation of our love. After a superb, toe-curling climax, we both collapsed as the waves of ecstasy swept over us. "Happy Birthday, Darling" she said proudly.

"That was a wonderful birthday present. Thank you, love." I was relieved that the phone had remained silent during love-making and wondered how I would have responded had a client phoned with a complex technical problem. We dressed, returned to the office and continued with some work for a little while. Carol, unfortunately, could not stay all day and had to leave mid-afternoon.

This strange relationship of ours which alternated between emotional extremes took another turn the very day after my birthday. Carol had a date with another man and told me in advance of meeting him. This gave me a harrowing evening as I jealously imagined her with someone else. My power of concentration was reduced to nothing and I found it impossible to do anything useful. I wished that I was not so much in love with someone who was constantly hurting me by seeking another man to replace me. It came as a relief when Carol phoned at eleven thirty. She had found the man pleasant, but not the type she wanted. We both became quite emotionally upset as we realised the irony of the situation. She assured me that I had nothing to fear and that she really did love me. For how long, I wondered? It could only be safe until she met someone who matched her requirements.

We saw each other on the Friday of that same week, when Carol arrived at my place in the afternoon. This was the last of our weekend breaks which I had organised. This time it was quite local and really was intended as an entertaining, indulgent weekend in Manchester. We left Carol's car at my house and drove into the city centre in my SAAB. We went into Piccadilly

Garden's area and, from there, drove up the spiral ramp into the roof top car park. We had dined at the Piccadilly hotel's restaurant several times, but this was to be our first overnight stay. Carol filled in the registration form as Mr. and Mrs. Raynor. We were disappointed to find that the room allocated to us had not been cleaned and the bedding unchanged since the last occupant. An indignant call to reception seemed to have the desired effect and another room was quickly provided.

Once we had unpacked, the need for each other's body overwhelmed us. Surrendering to these erotic desires, we undressed, caressed, kissed and made beautiful love. I always felt that what we did was not just having sex, as our souls seemed to touch during intercourse. It always gave so much pleasure to both of us and I could not imagine life without these sensational unions of minds and bodies.

The leisure centre in the basement of the hotel was our next call. For nearly an hour we exercised in the swimming pool. Although I was now a lot more confident in the water, Carol was a far better swimmer than me, but we still both enjoyed ourselves. Back in our room, we had a snack which Carol had brought. This was to serve as our evening meal, since I had booked for the evening performance of 'Les Miserables' at the Palace Theatre. It was good to see how popular live theatre still was. The musical of the famous story had been running for many months and was still packed out. It was a long show, lasting for over three hours, but we both enjoyed it immensely. A ten minute walk from the theatre, on a pleasant, August evening, brought us back to our hotel.

We loved sleeping together. Even if we did not have intercourse, it was so comforting just to lie naked together. We would both lie on our side, Carol with her back to my chest. This would allow me to put one arm around her, with my hand caressing and holding her breasts. Next morning, after making love, we had a light breakfast and spent a while in the swimming pool.

It was when we came to check out of the hotel, that we hit a problem. Carol could not find the car keys, no matter how hard she looked. After a while, we realised what had happened.

When we had arrived, she had put the keys down in the first room which had not been cleaned. Carol went with a porter to look in this room, but returned empty-handed. The only conclusion we could reach was that the chambermaid had picked up the keys, but had forgotten to hand them in. Since she was not on duty that day we still had a problem of how to drive away from the hotel.

The only solution I could think of, was to go back home to pick up my spare key. Carol felt most guilty and was surprised that I was not annoyed with her. Such things did not worry me and were certainly no reason to become angry. We caught the Metro-Link, Manchester's recently opened tram system and headed towards Altrincham. It was a simple, quick method of transport and, within an hour and a half, we had returned to the hotel armed with another key. In the meantime, the hotel had been in touch with the chambermaid and she had brought the key from home. Although, in effect, our journey had been unnecessary, we did not mind, since it was a pleasant, sunny day and we had plenty of spare time.

From there, we drove towards St. Peter's Square and our favourite hotel. At reception, we handed the car key to a porter who took the car to the hotel's car park for the night. The room was far superior to the one we had slept in for the previous night. We did not stay long, since we were now feeling quite hungry. A walk to Marks and Spencer's food hall provided plenty of tasty snacks. We sat in a little park at the side of Kendal's store, just off Deansgate, and enjoyed rolls, roast chicken, cakes and fruit. Once we had satisfied our hunger, we had a look around some of the shops along Deansgate, including Kendal's. Late afternoon, we returned to the hotel with our purchases. For the third time in twenty four hours, we then had a swim in the small pool at the leisure centre. Although it was smaller than the other hotel's pool, I was more used to it and felt quite comfortable. Carol did find the size a bit limiting, but enjoyed her swim just the same.

We both positioned ourselves to take best advantage of the strong, invigorating jets of water in the Jacuzzi, hoping, somehow, that they might melt away those spare bulges of fat. Again, we took advantage of the situation and touched each other intimately, obscured by the foaming water.

By far the biggest extravagance of this weekend was to be our evening meal. In contrast to our inexpensive picnic at lunchtime, I had booked a table in the French restaurant in our hotel, as we had done the previous November. It was certainly the most expensive restaurant in which I had ever dined, but, for a special occasion, it was well worth it. The relaxed, intimate surroundings, the excellent food and the company of the woman I loved all combined to make this a beautiful evening. I was more adventurous in choice of food, having wild boar for the main course, something I had never yet tried. Of course, Carol was able to sample this as well. We were very indulgent and had two bottles of wine between us.

Our indulgences did lead to us being more intoxicated than we had intended, but we enjoyed the evening immensely. It did mean that Carol was tired and not very amorous when we went to bed. We slept with our naked bodies pressed close together, but were awaken at three in the morning. The sound of champagne bottles being opened and laughter in the room above ours had disturbed our sleep. We listened to the celebrations for a little while and then took advantage of the disturbance. We began kissing and petting, while our legs began entwining around each other. By lightly kissing and sucking her nipples, I aroused strong sexual feelings in Carol and she urged me to penetrate her. The sounds of the party above us had now disappeared from my consciousness as we enjoyed each other's bodies. I felt certain that the people above us would not notice the sounds from the creaking bed or ourselves, but was not really bothered if they did.

"John, Darling, I love you so much." She sounded so genuine and sincere, that I really did believe her. We both fell into a satisfied sleep after reaching the pinnacle of our sexual desires.

When we awoke, later that morning, we had a most unusual breakfast. We had purposely left some food from our picnic on the previous day. There were fresh raspberries and apricots, which we enjoyed while sitting in bed, both of us still quite naked. There was something very juvenile in our actions, but it really did not seem to matter. For the last time, that weekend, we had a swim in the hotel's pool. This had been a superb weekend and I hoped that we could continue having such good times together for a long time to come.

It came as a terrible wrench when we had to part, later that afternoon. We had been together for forty eight hours. Forty eight wonderful, exciting and loving hours. I felt empty and desolate when Carol left me at my house. The sudden contrast emphasised my loneliness and I desperately hoped that Carol would change her mind and marry me. Over the weekend, she had said, several times, just how much she loved me, but would this be enough for her?

Only two days later, when I was talking to Carol early in the morning, she said that she was again thinking of driving to see Dave. After a lot of logical reasoning, she agreed that it would be a pointless, crazy thing to do. She was obviously going through deep, emotional torment and phoned me very early in the morning. I did not mind, since I had told her, many times, to phone me whenever she wanted, no matter what the hour.

I spent another anxious evening as Carol had yet another date with the man she had seen a couple of weeks earlier. When she did phone me, after returning from her date, she said that it was unlikely that they would be meeting again. Although I did feel relief at this, she made it quite clear that, when she was with someone else, she felt a deep sense of guilt because of the hurt it caused me. What else could I do but feel hurt, when the woman I loved was seeking someone else as a marriage partner?

"Perhaps we should stop seeing each other. Then you could meet other men without feeling guilty about me." As I was saying this, I was desperately hoping that she would not take up my suggestion. After all, our sixteen month relationship should be strong enough to give me some degree of security. I could not imagine that even Carol could just discard me after all we meant to each other.

My feelings were confirmed as she started crying and said, "Oh, John. Please don't leave me now. I need you so much."

I felt guilty for making the suggestion. "Don't worry, love. There is no way that I want to stop seeing you. You know how much I love you." She seemed comforted by my reassurances and became calmer.

Carol and I were due to go to the theatre on the following Saturday. She surprised me, by saying one night, that since her boys would be with us, that she did not want to hold hands with me in the theatre as we usually did. Why this simple act of affection should cause her embarrassment, I could not imagine. After all the boys had known about us sleeping together while in Paris, so they would probably be even more surprised if we did not show some affection to each other.

I next saw Carol on the Friday of that same week. She and the boys arrived shortly after mid-day. We all drove into Manchester and headed for Liverpool Road, just off Deansgate. Our destination, that day, was the Museum of Science and Industry. There are many places worth seeing in Manchester and this is certainly one of them. We spent quite a while in one room where there were many scientific experiments designed in such a way as to be easily understood and entertaining, especially for children. In another room, a very old mechanical loom was still in full working order and being demonstrated. Outside, there were actual steam locomotives near to another building which housed working mill engines. The boys particularly enjoyed walking through a simulation of a Victorian sewer, complete with examples of ancient lavatories and sanitary fittings. The afternoon ended with a walk around the Aviation centre, where Peter and Martin enjoyed trying the flight simulator.

We returned to my home, where Carol made a meal for us all.

I enjoyed this family atmosphere and had become quite attached to Carol's boys. I knew I would have no difficulty in accepting them as my own if Carol and I were to marry. After our meal, we left the boys watching television while Carol and I went for a walk.

Carol did know that, as with everybody else in the current recession, my business was going through a difficult time. I knew I could keep the company going, but said to her, "After this weekend, we will have to spend a bit less on our outings, love. I need to budget carefully during this awful recession."

She squeezed my arm in a comforting gesture and said, "Don't worry about it, darling. I understand."

"The trouble is that I want to spend money on you. I love to spoil you and give you treats."

"I know you do, John, but we can be more economic when we see each other. If you come to my house one weekend and I come to yours the next, we can still enjoy ourselves. I can make the meals and we can stay in watching videos."

"Are you sure you don't mind, Carol?" I did not want to lose her love and hoped that she could still accept me without all the extravagances I had showered on her over the past sixteen months.

"No, I don't mind and you must try and stop spoiling me." She gave me a kiss of assurance.

"We can still go to the theatre, but perhaps less often. And, in future, we should take the boys with us, if it's something they would enjoy."

"That's a good idea, John. You really are prepared to accept them, aren't you?"

"Of course. They are your children and have every right to expect some attention." She gave me another squeeze and we headed back for my house. I had suggested that they all stay at my place, since we were all to go to the theatre the very next day. As expected, Carol had refused and drove back to North Wales that night.

Late afternoon on the Saturday, they all returned to my house.

We drove into Manchester and parked in the multi-storey park at the rear of the Law Courts. From there, we walked to the Opera House on Quay Street. The show we were to see was Agatha Christie's 'Witness for the Prosecution'. I had suggested this show because it was not too heavy for the boys. They had seen very little live theatre over the years and Carol had wanted them to see a production at Manchester's magnificent theatres. We all enjoyed the play and Martin, in particular, was spellbound. I was pleased that the night was turning out to be a success. In the event, Carol and I did hold hands and, provided it was not too open, she allowed me to show some degree of affection.

When we left the theatre around ten, we walked towards St. Peter's Square. The other treat for the boys was to have a meal in our favourite hotel. This time, however, it was to be the Wyvern Restaurant, where I suggested that the boys cook their own meal. I do not think they really believed me until the waitress confirmed that they could cook meats at the table on hot stones. The boys thought this a great idea and enjoyed themselves, turning the thin slices of meat on the sizzling hot stone. Carol and I had chosen a more conventional menu and the evening passed without a hitch. It was almost midnight before we started our journey back to my home. They did not stay long and set off for the drive back, once more.

When I suggested that they all stay with me overnight, she said there was not much point, as they still had to drive the journey some time. I had merely wanted to extend the time together as much as possible. I did ask Carol when we could next meet, thinking that, perhaps next time, I could spend the weekend at Carol's as she had said the day before.

I was surprised when she said, "I don't know, but it can't be next week." I did not ask what she was doing, but I was yet to discover the relevance behind Carol's reply. In fact, the whole weekend was to become yet another landmark in our turbulent relationship.

When I phoned Carol late on Sunday evening, she was not in,

much to my surprise. She telephoned me shortly before midnight and confessed to meeting another man. She told me that they had been to a pub together and that this was the first day they had met or spoken. She thought she might grow to like him although he did not have the magical effect on her she had hoped for. In fact, she said he seemed to have a chip on his shoulder. Why was she so desperately trying to find someone else, when we had become so close? Although I was hurt, I did feel fairly confident that she would soon tire of him and return to me.

It came as a shock when Carol told me that she had a date to see this man on Tuesday evening. They would be going to a restaurant in Chester, much to my despair. When she telephoned me on her return, my anxiety deepened when she told me they were to meet again, within a matter of days. The worry of losing Carol very quickly affected my health. I found it impossible to sleep and felt physically sick. I had no appetite and concentration became more and more difficult.

Carol did say that she was thinking of Dave all the time she was with this new man, who, in fact, had the same Christian name as me. This did not lessen my anxiety, since it obviously had not stopped her from seeing him again. If she had said that she was thinking of me while she was with him, that would have offered a little consolation, but, at times like this, Carol could be ruthless and hurtful in what she said. I had always encouraged her to tell me the truth, but she did not seem to regard my feelings as being of any importance.

One of the worst aspects of these problems was to discover how Carol had lied to me. When I had asked her, the previous Saturday, how soon I could see her, she had told me that it could not be the following Saturday. She now revealed to me that she was seeing this other man on that day. According to Carol, the first time she had spoken to him was on the Sunday which would have been impossible, since she must already have made her date. When I asked her to explain this inconsistency, she could not and admitted that it had been a lie. She had actually spoken to him several days earlier and had obviously made a 'block' booking of three dates.

With this exposure, it revealed that her assurances of our continued relationship had all been lies. Her suggestion of spending alternate weekends at each other's houses and keeping down costs could only have been made without any real conviction. The only excuse she could offer was that she did not want to hurt me. Although I found the pain hard to bear, Carol had hurt me so much over the time we had known each other that I had almost come to expect it of her. Her memory was not as good as mine and certainly not good enough to be consistent with her lies.

Our telephone conversations became a bit strained after these exchanges and I felt absolutely devastated and cheated by her. I was thoroughly exhausted and very confused. One fact of which I was certain was the realisation that, if Carol was capable of deceiving me so much, then she was not the woman I would want to marry. I knew that I had been a better friend to her than anybody else she had either known in the past or likely to meet in the future and, yet, this obviously counted for nothing. No man was safe with such an uncaring, selfish, untrustworthy woman. Even with my intimate knowledge of her, I had underestimated how ruthless she could be. Despite all this, my love and desire for her had not diminished in the slightest, causing me a great deal of emotional torture.

In this confused and desperate state of mind, I tried to work out just what alternatives faced me. My situation seemed so hopeless that I, once again, thought of committing suicide. I spent many, lonely hours in tears, looking for any possible solution to my problems. My eyes stung from the pain of my distress and I searched my mind for someone I could phone for support. The only people I could easily contact were, like my parents, the ones who I was determined should not know of my situation. It was then that an idea, a tiny glimmer of hope, came to mind. I was a firm believer in the power of the paranormal after many years of conclusive evidence. I contacted a local reliable psychic, Roger Dorset, hoping that I could see him that day, but he was not able to come until the next day, Sunday.

When Carol did call me after her date, she made it quite clear that I had now become an embarrassment to her. She was obviously hoping that she may grow to love him. "I don't think we should see each other again, John." This statement, although not unexpected, hurt me so much, it took my breath away.

"But, why? You've only known this man for a week and you're prepared to throw away everything we have built up over the last sixteen months?"

"I want a clean sheet, John. I must be honest with him and I can't do that if I'm still seeing you." It seemed ironic that I had encouraged her to tell the truth and now she was using this against me. To make it worse, she had told me lies at the same time she was professing to be honest.

It was only a couple of weeks earlier when she had pleaded with me not to leave her when she needed me most. Needless to say, I had not let her down. "I need you now, more than at any other time, Carol. Is there no way you can still see me?"

"I can't, John. It wouldn't be right. We can still speak to each other on the phone."

"That's not much consolation. It's like serving me an appetiser in a restaurant and then taking the main course to the man on the next table." If the analogy amused her, she did not laugh, but did accept my point. We were both upset and felt that nothing constructive could be achieved by continuing the conversation.

That night was one of the worst in my life. Her actions caused me such pain, that I wished she had just shot me, since it could not have been more painful. When the psychic arrived the following morning, I told him nothing of my reason for calling him. He knew nothing at all of my background and I hid any objects which may lead to him making guesses about my life.

He asked me to shuffle Tarot cards and cut the pack. I had then to remove one card and place it on the table. What he told me after that was as a result of reading the cards and interpreting psychic messages.

"I see two women in your life. One is from the past, but was a very long, sometimes difficult relationship, possibly a marriage. I'm surprised that you stayed with her as long as you did." I said nothing and was determined not to give him any clues. "Now the other woman is very interesting. She's very close to you, although something, some rift seems to have happened recently." I still did not respond, since everything so far could be conjecture. I was stunned by what he said next. "She has, not very long ago, been involved in a car accident. The car was very badly damaged, but she came out of it okay. She was a very lucky woman." There was no way he could have known this by guessing. He had to be genuine. "I can see her with lots of flowers. She's a woman who likes gardening and arranging flowers. You have come to a crossroads with this woman and unsure about what to do."

I nodded in agreement as tears filled my eyes. I could not help sobbing as the whole tragic situation became so transparent to this complete stranger. "I know you are very much in love with her, but, believe me, you are better off without her. There is another man in her life, but it isn't someone recent. He has had an influence on her for several years, now. He appears as the Emperor, but the card shows him with a crossed sword. This means that, although they had a very strong bond, it was a relationship that could never word. Right from the start, it was destined to fail. The sad thing is, he has spoiled her and she will spend the rest of her life searching for the special feeling she had for this man with others. She will never find it."

It was incredible that he could even see Dave in what was becoming a fascinating revelation. "She will come back to you, but don't let her drag you down, again. Whatever you do, don't go to North Wales." He even knew her location! How on earth...? He continued "As for you, you have no need to worry. You have a long and healthy life in front of you. There are two women, one of whom you have yet to meet. Both of them feel very strongly about you. One, in particular, is very beautiful and has a definite ethnic look to her. That cheek bone structure is superb. You'll be alright. In fact, you're a very lucky man." He smiled and I had a distinct impression that he was envious of me having such future women friends to lighten my life.

"There is another woman, who you have already met. She lives in Europe and looks as though she could be Dutch. I feel certain that she will stay in contact with you for many years. I don't see a marriage there, but a very good friend." This could be nobody else but Mirz Braams from Amsterdam and I was relieved that we were going to remain friends. Roger Dorset had told me everything I needed to know and, as we had reached the end of his reading, he shook my hand and wished me a happy future before leaving me on my own again.

I sat quietly for a while, thinking of everything I had been told by this remarkable man. My spirits were raised by his observations. Really, he had confirmed what I had thought about Carol for some time. I knew she was not good enough for me and would probably never find happiness with anyone. In fact, she had even said this herself many times. The relief came in the possibility of me finding love with another woman. His description suggested that I would find a lasting relationship with one of my many pen friends from abroad. This, together with a seemingly healthy life, convinced me that I had, after all, something worth living for. I knew then, what I must do about Carol. Although we had said, on many occasions, that we would stay in contact for the rest of our lives, no matter what happened. This had now become an unrealistic ambition. If I was to succeed in a permanent, rewarding relationship with another woman, I had no choice but to stop any further communication with Carol. All ties had to be severed, however much pain this may cause.

It was late on Monday evening, the last day in August, nineteen ninety two when Carol phoned me. This had to be the time for decisive action. "Are you still certain that you will not see me again?" I asked, nervously. I was certain of her answer.

"I'm sorry, John. I don't think I should see you again. I must have a new start." She did sound genuinely sorry, but it did not lessen the degree of pain and ruthlessness she was using against me. The only crime I was guilty of was loving her too much.

"In that case, somehow I've got to get over you. And I'm not going to do that while we are still talking on the phone every day."

"You want me to stop phoning you?" I felt certain that she must have expected this response from me.

"It's not what I had wanted but it's the only way, Carol. I don't know how the hell I'm going to get over you, but somehow I've got to." Neither of us could conceal the emotion in our voices as we realised that this was to be the last ever phone call after a sixteen month marriage of souls. "You know, Carol. You have been both the best and the worst thing in my life. Take care of yourself, sweetheart. Goodbye."

A message from John Raynor, the author :

I can honestly say that this sixteen month period of my life was the most traumatic, alternating between the supreme highs of sexual satisfaction and the worst depressions I have ever experienced. All this was determined by my relationship with one woman, Carol. The events are accurate and the only changes are the true identities of Carol, her family, friend and former lover. I have not had contact with her since August, 1992 and hope that she succeeded in her quest for a suitable soul-mate in her life.

Epilogue

If the reader would like to find out how my own life fared after this turbulent period and how accurate the psychic's predictions were, this can be discovered by reading my subsequent autobiographical work, "Who wants to be British?", which is due to be published during June, 2012.

J. S. Raynor : November, 2011

Lightning Source UK Ltd.
Milton Keynes UK
UKOW040044120812

197434UK00003B/4/P